My Season on the Kenai

MY SEASON ON THE
KENAI

Fishing Alaska's Greatest Salmon River

Lew Freedman

A

ALASKA
NORTHWEST
BOOKS®

Library of Congress Cataloging-in-Publication Data

Freedman, Lew.
  My season on the Kenai : fishing Alaska's greatest salmon river / Lew Freedman.
    pages cm
    ISBN 978-0-88240-962-7 (hardbound)
    ISBN 978-0-88240-906-1 (pbk.)
    ISBN 978-0-88240-951-1 (e-book)
  1. Salmon fishing—Alaska—Kenai River. 2. Kenai River Region (Alaska) —
Description and travel. 3. Freedman, Lew—Travel. I. Title.
  SH686.F74 2013
  799.17'560979835—dc23
                    2013007806

Design by Rudy Ramos

Front cover photo: © iStockphoto.com/Jonathan Nafzger

Published by Alaska Northwest Books®
An imprint of Graphic Arts Books
P.O. Box 56118
Portland, Oregon 97238-6118
503-254-5591
www.graphicartsbooks.com

I would like to dedicate this story about the Kenai River to the late Harry Gaines, who helped develop my love of the river and Reuben Hanke, who keeps Harry's name alive on the river.

This carving of the late Harry Gaines overlooks the Kenai River at the Harry Gaines fish camp operated by Reuben Hanke.

Contents

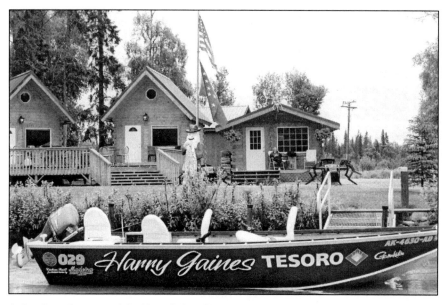

A view from the water of the Harry Gaines fish camp operated by guide Reuben Hanke.

Acknowledgments

Special thanks for all the help provided to make my summer work out so well go to Harry Gaines Kenai River Fishing owner Reuben Hanke, Fenton Brothers guides Mike and Murray Fenton, Alaska Fishing Service guide Kevin Thurman, Kenai River advocate Bob Penney, Ricky Gease, executive director of the Kenai River Sportfishing Association, and the Alaska Department of Fish and Game.

Weigh master David "Wahoo" Cole at the September 2012 Kenai River Women's Classic.

Introduction

When the water looks turquoise under a bright sun, with splashes of light glowing on the surface like diamonds as it rolls past, the Kenai River delights and hypnotizes me with its beauty. At those moments the river seems all dressed up for a special occasion, the coronation of a king maybe.

Those are the peaceful moments, when I am a bystander, an observer, just soaking in the sight of the dazzling river that is my favorite body of water in the world. One of the gems of Alaska, the Kenai is the world's greatest salmon stream, a picturesque, glacially fed river of both power and grace that is stunning in the way it combines its natural wildness with accessibility to man.

Located in Southcentral Alaska, the Kenai River is the jewel of the Kenai Peninsula, in some places situated only one hundred road miles from Anchorage, the forty-ninth state's largest city. The aboriginal Dena'ina called the river *Kakny*. A national treasure that attracts visitors from all over the world, it is also one of the most popular playgrounds for Alaskans who love to fish. Stretching eighty-two miles from the mouth of Cook Inlet, where the salmon enter from their Pacific Ocean travels, to Kenai Lake in Cooper Landing, the Kenai River is a sinuous waterway wending past aspens, spruce, and birch.

I was introduced to the Kenai River by reputation after moving to Alaska in 1984. Conversation, the stories of big fish and lucky fishermen, captivated me. Although I was not much of a fisherman then, deprived as I was by a big-city upbringing and a lack of family connected to the sport, it did not take much secondhand exposure to lure me in.

A complete novice waiting to be hooked, I asked around and was told that if I was going to fish on the Kenai River and attempt to wrangle a salmon into my boat, I needed to look up a personable guide named Harry Gaines. Gaines, I was told, could read the river like the lines on the palm of his hand, and he was a wizened old-timer with more experience than almost anyone else in the Soldotna-Kenai area, where most guides were based. About 150 miles from Anchorage, this area featured cozy, smaller cities along the banks of the Lower River.

The Lower River is where the king salmon, the most prized of all types of salmon, return to spawn each spring and summer, and where the angler with ambition goes to catch one. Kings, better known to the outside world as Chinook salmon, are the bad boys of the river, the big, even monstrous fish, that are difficult to entice onto a hook, that fight like hell when caught, and that offer delectable dinners when served.

The kings are the kings of the river. The biggest kings in the world return to the Kenai and this was proven year after year when fishermen and their guides were left agog as someone hooked into a hog of a fish weighing ninety pounds or more. For the typical fisherman, weaned on the sport in the rest of the United States, a big fish might be a five-pound bass, a common fish a perch, walleye, or bluegill weighing anywhere from a few ounces to a couple of pounds. Catching one of the giant king salmon (nobody even bothered to keep one that weighed less than thirty-five pounds) was the equivalent of hooking your fifth-grade son and trying to haul him into the boat.

As it so happened, within a year after my move to Alaska, a modest Soldotna car salesman named Les Anderson made fishing history one magical May day in 1985. Early one morning out with a buddy in a small boat, Anderson's hook was grabbed by a curious fish that bit hard into his offering and bent the pole almost double.

The fight was on and when Anderson prevailed after a mighty struggle he had caught the fish of every man's dreams. It weighed ninety-seven and one-quarter pounds and it represented a new world-record Chinook salmon caught on rod and reel.

Back in those days big kings were common, but no fish was larger and few approached the size of the dream fish. That did not deter guide Harry Gaines, who sported a white beard, a twinkle in his eye, and a background in radio broadcasting. He figured that Anderson's fish was the greatest advertisement for the Kenai River short of an appearance by the Loch Ness Monster's twin brother.

Sometime before I met him, Harry sought to turn Anderson's good fortune into his own, as well, with an advertising campaign that essentially was, "Come Fish with Me, Catch the World-Record Salmon, and Win $50,000." Harry was pledging a prize of fifty grand if you caught a world-record king fishing with him. At least that was the idea. He had to back off when Lloyd's of London refused to insure him. I never could believe that Lloyd's of London was too chicken to back that deal. Don't they insure anything? Anyway, out of prudence and respect for his bank account, Harry reduced his prize offering to $5,000. The gimmick lost some of its luster when that zero was dropped.

In any case, I finally went king salmon fishing with Harry. He was an entertaining guy. Good teller of jokes, corny and otherwise. Harry, originally from Texas, developed a special scent that when added to the shiny red salmon-egg bait in common use was supposed to be irresistible to a fish with a discerning palate. He also a believed in talking to the fish and requested that those who shared his boat participate in his fish cheer. "Give me an F, give me an I, give me an S, give me an H. What's that spell?"

Actually for me mostly it spelled no fish. I did not catch a king salmon with Harry my first time out. They apparently did not speak my language. Dutifully I wrote of my experience in the sports pages of the *Anchorage Daily News*, where I was then sports editor. Over the next couple of years I returned to the river regularly, always fishing with Harry because I had not yet caught a king salmon under his guidance and I felt it only fair that after publicizing our failures together I publicize our successes together.

I was a wise guy in the newspaper and Harry was a wise guy on the air as a couple of Kenai summer fishing seasons passed without me coming any closer to seeing a salmon than checking out cans in the grocery store. I was going salmon-less, but there were other perks. Not only did Harry and I become good friends—he definitely was amusing company—but I developed an abiding love for the river. Harry used to joke that people went salmon fishing with him because they wanted to catch fish, not because they liked boat rides. But I really enjoyed the boat rides, too. The river was its own world, so close to civilization, yet far enough removed to offer serenity. Sometimes eagles flew overhead. Sometimes seals popped up downstream. Sometimes moose swam the river's width. Once in a great while we saw a bear half-hidden in the trees on shore.

Eventually, I did catch fish with Harry, but we kept on fishing together, anyway. In 1990 Harry was stricken with a fast-moving cancer. The following spring, as he was dying, the local radio station recorded retrospective interviews with him reviewing his long career as a pioneer guide on the river and the changes he had seen since the 1970s. When asked to name the worst fisherman he had ever guided, Harry didn't hesitate. "Lew Freedman!" he said with enthusiasm. He probably figured he owed me that one from all of my strike-out columns. Besides, I laughed. I didn't hold it against him.

When Harry died in the summer of 1991, his ashes, appropriately, were spread in the Kenai River right near the fish-camp property he shared for years with his wife, Dot. One of the last things Harry said to me, less than two days before he passed away, was "Our memories remain forever."

He was right about that. Partially because of my friendship with Harry Gaines, my passion for the Kenai River never waned. For the last twenty-five years, I have made annual pilgrimages to the river, even after moving out of Alaska. Yet it was never enough. I wanted to spend more time on the river and during the summer of 2012 I was able to work life its ownself around so that I could devote an entire season to the Kenai.

My season was defined basically as the first week in April to the first week in October. During the course of these six months the Kenai shed its icy coat from winter, welcomed back the annual migration of king salmon; served as hospitable passageway for red, or sockeye, salmon by the hundreds of thousands; silver, or coho salmon; and pink, or humpy salmon. The pinks return by the million every other year in even-numbered years.

That's just salmon. The Kenai is also home to Dolly Varden and some of the most spectacular rainbow trout in the world.

There are almost as many different techniques for catching fish, from boats and banks, from fly casting to back trolling, as there are fish. For those of us who like boat rides, we can zoom up and down certain segments of the river at twenty miles per hour or so. For those who eschew motors, the Upper River has a rule against them, and it's possible to float in rubber rafts and catch fish.

In world-famous photographs documenting the phenomenon each year the Russian River tributary of the Kenai River becomes a temporary, but very convenient site for anglers anxious to catch reds. The fishermen stand elbow to elbow wearing waders in what would otherwise be prohibitively ice-cold water and try to hook fish instead of one another. This is jokingly described as "combat fishing."

Those who try to catch reds almost always are fishing on their own or with friends. They don't use boats and they don't rely on guides, but mainly on their own experience, learning from past trial and error (and following the hordes) where and when to go.

The river is not only for those who sportfish. For Alaskans who simply wish to feed their families there is a subsistence fishery. The head of the household can net fish by the dozen, depending on the size of the family. This is not about fishing for fun as much as it is filling the freezer for the long winter months ahead.

The quietest, least-used segment of the Kenai is the Middle River. It is a hybrid as far as on-water travel and boat versus bank fishing, with different rules for different areas, but most importantly that's where those oversized rainbow trout hover.

Upper River, Middle River, Lower River, king salmon fishing, silver fishing, red fishing, rainbow trout fishing, rafting, for one summer, for one Kenai River fishing season, I was determined to do it all.

I spent time with family (daughter and grandsons). I spent time with a longtime guide friend, Reuben Hanke, who succeeded Harry Gaines, but out of friendship and respect has kept his mentor's name on the business. I met many new people who absorb joy from the river in so many ways. And I stumbled into unexpected events that impacted the return of certain salmon, kicking off an outcry of worry, and jump-starting a lesson in fish politics.

When the season began, the unknown was part of the attraction. There were major events scheduled on the Kenai River over the summer, locked into calendar positions, and I checked them all out. But just as you never know what kind of fish and what size fish might be tugging on your line when the rod bends, you never know what kind of excitement awaits during a season on the Kenai River.

It was an unforgettable season for me, sampling so much of what the river offered. It is easy to understand how for many Alaskans, and for many visitors, the Kenai River is that most special place on earth that they cherish. I was one of them before the season began and I remain one of them now.

—Lew Freedman
December 2012

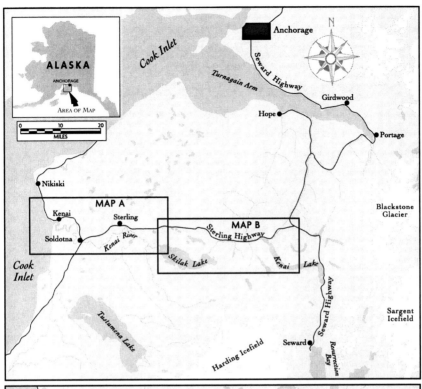

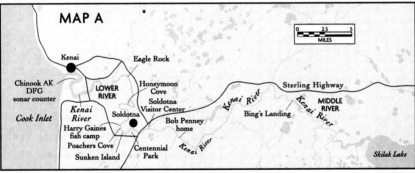

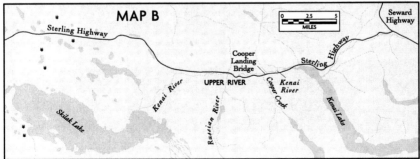

Britain Willis, six, one of my grandsons, went fishing for king salmon for the first time in his life on the Kenai River in July of 2012, but didn't catch one.

April

OPEN WATER

The sky was thick with dense, gray clouds in some areas, while sun fought to shine through in others. Snow lined the banks, hard snow that crunched when you walked across it. Patches of ice seeped out from land, thin ice, fall-through-the-ice mirage ice. It was just solid enough to make a cracking sound as you fell in. But there was open water. The Kenai River was open for business.

Men wearing waders and carrying fishing rods dotted the shore over a one-hundred-yard stretch at the headwaters of the Kenai, where it spills into Kenai Lake at Cooper Landing, one hundred miles from Anchorage. They were diehards.

It would be no surprise to find Alaska's most popular salmon stream frozen solid on the first day of April, but these gamblers drew winning lottery tickets. Water, not ice, showed beneath the Cooper Landing Bridge and if there was water, there were fish.

Snow covered most of the boat launch area, but an angler watching his step could scope out a spot and throw a line into the green, glittering waters of the Kenai and hope. The Kenai is fed by glacial melt and when it is exposed in sunshine the color is something akin to turquoise or gentle green. Anyone who has seen Miami under the sun has seen the Atlantic Ocean glowing in the same manner.

That color mesmerizes. It is like walking into a jewelry shop and being struck blind by a necklace that you have to have for your loved one. When you see it you are helpless. When you see it you are lured by it. It is one way the Kenai River touches people in their soul. That may sound gushy romantic, but nature sometimes teases us that way. There are moments we walk into a panorama so beautiful, so wild, so intensely carved from the earth that we are enraptured. We are reminded that the earth we inhabit has locations prettier than any we can make and that it features places much bigger and more powerful than we are. When we happen upon one of these places we don't want to leave, yet feel comforted that when we do it will always be there as is when we come back.

The Kenai River is such a place for Alaskans, for fishermen, and for visitors who have heard and learned so much about it that the river has taken on mythological proportions. One fact gives this image a monumental boost. In 1985, the world-record king salmon was caught on rod and reel in the Kenai. It weighed ninety-seven and one-quarter pounds, so large that it is the ultimate fish of dreams, and many dream of catching its big brother.

But the Kenai River is many things to many people, from scenic painting to fisherman's paradise. On a nippy day in April, it just makes people happy by showing itself.

Spring in Alaska is a tug-of-war between chill and warmth, between flipping the page on the calendar and the pages being stuck together. Winter never surrenders easily. Unlike the rest of the United States, where spring announces its arrival with new growth, grass turning green, plants flowering, days where the temperatures are high enough to make anyone wearing a coat sweat, in Alaska the struggle is sometimes brutal. A sneak attack may bring a late blizzard. Hard frosts may hang on. In Alaska the entire season is characterized by one thing—breakup. Breakup is meltdown. It means the snow that has been piling up on the ground since October finally goes away. It may well disappear grudgingly, shrinking inch by inch in the reverse process of how it was added, until one day you wake up and realize the snow is gone except for that patch over there in the shade. Sometimes breakup strikes with a vengeance and you can practically swim in the streets. There are puddles and there are mini-floods. When you encounter that you know it is spring.

To be truthful, spring may really only last a week, the transition from winter to summer happening in an eyeblink. You turned your head and missed spring altogether. The Kenai River may endure similar stages. There may be open water during the day, but freeze-up all over again at night. Once that happens it's only a matter of time until all of the ice fades. The river is in transition, transforming from an eighty-two-mile-long block of ice into a swiftly flowing body of water once again.

Eighty-two miles. That is the length of the Kenai River, from Kenai Lake to the mouth of Cook Inlet, the body of water named for Captain James Cook, the British explorer who came calling on Alaska on the third and last of his seafaring journeys in 1778 before he perished in Hawaii in 1779. Cook Inlet is the gateway to the Pacific Ocean. A statue of the captain stands in downtown Anchorage, up the coastline from the Kenai River at the other end of Cook Inlet at Turnagain Arm. Kenai Lake is in the Kenai Mountains and the river passes through the Kenai National Wildlife Refuge.

Throughout the centuries writers have employed the metaphor describing snow-bound landscapes as being asleep. Well, when frozen completely in the middle of a winter when the temperature hits minus twenty, the Kenai River has definitely nodded off. You can say it's gone on vacation, but hibernation would be more accurate. At the most extreme periods of winter it pretty much ceases to be a river, at least as we know it.

But now there was water again. On the drive from Anchorage on the Seward Highway, and then the Sterling Highway, I had wondered what I would find. I hoped for the sight of some open water, but I expected to see a frozen river, pretty much covered in snow, especially following a winter of record snowfall where about 140 inches of flakes had accumulated. My assumption was that I was approaching a desolate river.

Wrong. Swinging around the bend in the road where the Cooper Landing Bridge crosses the Kenai I saw water. I grinned, pleased just to catch a glimpse of river. Then, to my surprise, I saw a fisherman walking up the path from the river, heading home. Then to my right I saw others. To my left, I saw still more fishermen. Where there is water there is opportunity.

I caught up to Carl Locke. He is from Seward, more than fifty miles away from this spot. Dressed warmly in layers he thought it was worth it to chase rainbow trout on a Sunday afternoon. "I had to get out of the house," he said.

Locke, sixty-two, was no novice fisherman. There were fish to be had, but not without work. There might be silver salmon, cohos, or even a whitefish out there that could be enticed onto a hook, he figured. But not this day, not for Locke.

"Not a thing," he said of his take-home catch. "It's hit and miss." His previous time out, he hit. "You can catch some nice fish. I had a twenty-five-incher (rainbow trout) last weekend." How cold is too cold to come out? "I draw the line at about twenty degrees."

That is one difference between real Alaskan fishermen and Lower 48 fishermen. The definition of what is too cold to function with a rod in hand may vary. Indeed, it may vary by thirty degrees. To exist without being a hermit in Alaska one must adapt to the notion that it is a cold-weather place. If that bothers you, you should move, or you would never go out of the house. Still, for some fishing when the temperatures are in the twenties is where the line is drawn. Call me back when it's in the forties, they might say.

For others, perhaps there is even a macho sense at work that they are conquering the elements, not letting the weather tell them what to do. It can be as simple as this: See water, fish water. Everything else is extraneous.

Zach Tomco, twenty-six, of Palmer, about two hundred miles away, had fished on the Kenai River for ten years for king salmon, but never so early in the year. "You just dress for it," he said casually when asked if he was cold. Dressing for the weather meant wearing neoprene waders, a good, sturdy coat, and a hat, maybe with earflaps. Not just Tomco, but for the others nearby, too.

Tomco was here on the river in April because he had never been on the river in April and "you always hear about it." He heard you can catch fish if there is enough open water and if you don't care that you are courting frostbite on your fingers. Sacrifices must be made.

Tomco, Locke, and another half-dozen souls fishing this stretch of the Kenai on this day seemed prepared to make them. You had to love fishing, you had to love the river, to go out when common sense told you that the odds were slim you would catch anything besides a cold.

I moved on, following the bends in the Sterling Highway as the pavement tracked the curves of the river, but I only saw snow and ice and I never saw

In early April, hard-core fishermen were able to find open water on the Kenai River near the Cooper Landing Bridge, but there was still plenty of snow and ice around.

another fisherman. It was quiet. There were few cars on the road. The birch and spruce, trees that did not lose leaves in winter, were tall, slender, and tightly bunched. A moose darted across the highway, a common enough occurrence in Southcentral Alaska, in a frightened sprint. I was the one who should have been frightened. Moose win most collisions with small cars.

An eagle was perched on a downed tree at the side of the road, facing the tiny Cooper Landing business district. Snow patches abounded, but they were patches, not huge berms. Pretty soon all of the Kenai River would be open, the water running freely once more. But for a small sampling of anglers the fishing season had already begun.

THE GREAT ALASKA SPORTSMAN SHOW

On the same weekend in Anchorage, the fishing season was beginning in a completely different way—indoors at Sullivan Arena, its parking lot, and adjacent Ben Boeke Arena. This four-day event, held annually since 1984, is where people went that were getting ready for the fishing season, but were not quite prepared to venture outdoors in the great outdoors.

Searching for a new fishing rod, reel, line, lures, outer apparel, extra-warm underwear, hats, boots, boats, you name it, in this temporary one-stop outdoors shopping mecca is part of the ritual of getting ready. Every fisherman knows that he must need some new gizmo that he doesn't yet know exists before he can go fishing again. Last year's stuff is so passé.

The massive show, which attracts thousands and thousands of visitors, has grown steadily since its inception. At one time it was confined to the walls of Sullivan Arena, the 7,000-seat civic arena most often used as a venue for hockey. But as demand increased, vendor interest soared, and the outdoorsmen kept on coming, the booths spilled out of Sullivan into a large tent squeezing parking spaces, and then filled out Ben Boeke, a smaller ice arena, across the parking lot.

Goods and services provided revolve around every aspect of the outdoors, not just fishing, and certainly the devoted hunter can find what he needs on the premises, too. But the show is held in April, when the state is gearing up for fishing season.

"If we were to break it down, the fishing category would be heaviest," said Steve Shepherd, one of the show's organizers and someone who has been involved with it from the start. "We're heavy on fishing, but also on rafting and hiking and hunting. There are more people who take advantage of the great outdoors now."

Shepherd, who is from Anchorage, like so many show attendees, is a Kenai River disciple. He journeys to the river every year, usually two or three times over the summer, and fishes for king salmon and silver salmon. The biggest king he has ever caught weighed forty-something pounds and only an Alaskan would observe that such a fish wasn't all that big.

"I've never been blessed with a really big one," Shepherd said.

However, his son Brian has been. About a half-dozen years ago when Brian was around thirteen, he caught a twenty-nine and seven-eighths-inch-long rainbow trout that the Shepherds really wanted to be thirty inches.

Shepherd fishes the Lower Kenai River for kings and the Upper Kenai River for rainbows, a stretch of water where no motorized boats are allowed.

"It's peaceful," he said. "I go back for the company, for the beauty. I pinch myself every time and I think it's good to be alive."

One thing the Sportsman Show is not is peaceful. Booths are crammed in tight, the crowds turn out in force, and there are human traffic jams in the aisles. If a visitor picked up a brochure for every booth and stockpiled all of the information made available from government agencies pushing tourism, and copies of the Alaska Department of Fish and Game's annual fishing regulations, plus reports of activities on the river, he could easily walk away with twenty pounds of paper.

The Kenai Peninsula Tourism Marketing Council, Inc. produced a sixty-page glossy magazine of advertising titled "Alaska's Playground: 2012 Kenai Peninsula Discovery Guide."

Although the Kenai River is the five-star attraction of the region, people may be lured to the communities of Kenai, Soldotna, Nikiski, Homer, Seward, Kasilof, Anchor Point, Clam Gulch, and elsewhere. They may fish in Resurrection Bay and on other lakes, streams, and rivers. They may participate in rafting, canoeing, boating, hiking, bear watching, flight-seeing and sightseeing, birding and beachcombing. They may fly in, bus in, Winnebago in, or drive themselves.

All worthy activities and a little variety for the family, but in all seriousness fishing on the Kenai River is what drives the economy. If king salmon fishing is slow, then it's not that challenging to find a hotel room. If red salmon rush through by the millions, you can't find a room.

While outdoors-related merchandise is for sale, as well as anything anyone might ever think to use in the outdoors, from flashlights to pen knives, from sunscreen to coolers, from easy-to-carry snacks to rough-and-ready meals, the meat-and-potatoes guys of the show are the guides.

The guides are selling, too. They are booking trips for the season. "Show Special!" a sign may scream at a booth. That means if you book early you get a discount. What might be a $175 trip normally can be transformed into a $150 trip. If you want to fish in May, which is really before the tourists find their way in bulk to airports, a special deal can be arranged.

Colored brochures displaying beautiful views of the river, gorgeous sunsets, and always, always smiling fishermen holding up the biggest honkers of king salmon that you ever laid eyes on are come-hither advertising that are designed to woo even the most hesitant planner into making a commitment.

It works, too. Year after year the same guides return, carrying day planners with blank pages and they depart the long weekend with pages of appointments for May, June, July, September. Frequently they book return customers, satisfied clients who come year after year to the same guide service, to fish with the same guides who have steered them right in the past.

The wanderer can fill a bulging bag with such brochures, or business cards, representing guide services trying to sell essentially the same service: Come with us and you'll catch fish. They must be pretty much telling the truth, too, or else they would have folded by now. Guides that don't find fish don't stay in business for the long run.

Fish are caught, friendships begin, clients are happy, and habits are formed. If you have a good time fishing with a certain guide and you catch fish it's hard to break the chains. Why would you? There is no guarantee the next guide will be as good. I understand this. My staple guide on the Kenai is Reuben Hanke. We were originally brought together by our mutual friend Harry Gaines, and Reuben bought Harry Gaines Kenai River Fishing. After Harry died I kept going to the same fish camp I had always gone to. That's going on twenty-five years now. If circumstances dictate I can only fish once a year on the Kenai River, or once a season, it's going to be with Reuben.

Still, variety can be fun sometimes and I filled my plastic carry bag with the advertisements of many guide services, including Fenton Brothers, Kenai River Charters, RW's Fishing, Kenai River Drifter's Lodge (located on the Upper River, their material reads, "It's All Down River From Here"), Alaska Wildland Adventures, Alaska Clearwater Sportfishing, Inc., and Phil's Smiling Salmon Guide Service.

I was particularly taken with Phil's business card. It pictures a human hanging upside down on a scale with a smiling salmon wearing a vest and balancing a fishing rod upright next to him.

In the course of my rounds, weaving in and out of the Sullivan Arena aisles, talking to people manning booths I have known for years, I met Kevin Thurman. The vast majority of my Kenai River fishing has been on the Lower River, where guides steer Evinrudes, Yamahas, or Mercuries from place to place trying to seize the moment at famously labeled fishing spots like Eagle Rock. Sometimes they zip around bends at thirty miles per hour or so.

By contrast, the Upper River does not permit the use of boats equipped with motors. The boats move with the current and with muscle power, as guides dip oars as they push and pull. This is a more tranquil experience, a different type of fishing. Fly fishermen tend to concentrate on the Upper River. Also, the big king salmon do not swim to the Upper River in numbers. They mass and spawn in the Lower River, so anglers on the Upper River concentrate on other species.

Thurman's operation was something different, something I was totally unfamiliar with, even after all of my years fishing on the Kenai. Thurman, fifty, is a sturdy block of a man, not too tall, but wide, with a mustache and beard going slightly gray. He looks as if he once played defensive tackle for some high school. What he's been doing for years is guiding the Middle Kenai River. The Middle River was a blank slate to me. It was neither here nor there.

"It's faster water than the Upper River," said Thurman, whose company is Alaska Fishing Service. "It's not as wide as the Lower River. There are a bunch of gravel bars and you can actually see the fish there when the water is low. When the water is high you can't see the gravel bars. That's why people lose props on their boats. You've got to know the river."

Thurman specialized in guiding on twelve miles of river between Skilak Lake to the north and Bings Landing to the south. Fishing with Thurman meant fishing for rainbow trout and Dolly Varden, and silver salmon and red salmon at times, too. Thurman's vessel was what he called a handmade "cataraft." It was basically a rubber raft stabilized by two hulls, a blending of a simple raft and a catamaran. It was almost surely the only boat of its kind on the Kenai.

Being on a comparatively secluded section of the river, Thurman said he sees few other people when he is fishing and at times with friends or clients he has had insane success in catching and then releasing rainbow trout. In one four-hour drift on a May trip with a friend covering over two miles of water Thurman said they caught one hundred rainbows. On an August trip with three clients, he said, they once hooked two hundred rainbows and red salmon.

I did not see any publicizing of those types of mind-boggling success stories in Kevin's brochure and mentioned that. "I don't want to get their expectations up," he said. Still, as we all know, there are no guarantees that if we go fishing we're going to catch fish. "We're not going to get skunked. It's all about the timing."

The Middle River. Wow, something new for me on the Kenai. "It's like a secret," Thurman said. "But the word is getting out."

Kevin Thurman guides on his handmade cataraft on the Middle River section of the Kenai River, frequently specializing in catching rainbow trout. He also ties his own flies.

Murray and Mike Fenton have been regulars at the Sportsman Show for years. Mike, fifty-three, and Murray, fifty-two, have actually set up in the same location in Sullivan Arena for years, by one of the exits. When the organizers asked if they wanted to upgrade to floor space in the middle of the action downstairs, they decided to stay right where they were. Their clients know where to find them.

"It's like old home week," said Mike as former customers walked up to their table to shake hands.

"This is the only show we do," Murray said.

It would be easy to fill winter months touring the Lower 48 states appearing at sportsman's shows in big cities like Chicago, Milwaukee, and Minneapolis, and at one time or another in their careers, most Alaska-based guides did the circuit, feeling they had to remind anglers the state was more than an abstract concept, but a real place where they could catch a fish of a lifetime if they tried their hand for king salmon on the Kenai River. Now it's a lot cheaper to throw up a website. A fisherman from another state with his mind on Alaska will search out what he's after. The Alaska show is pretty much for Alaskans who have been suffering from cabin fever and are itching to get outdoors. They may be impulse buyers, looking for their first Kenai River trip. For them the booths at this show represent a smorgasbord.

The Fenton brothers have been guiding for more than a quarter century and they have treated thousands of anglers to glorious fishing days on the Kenai River, some of them many times. Yet even some of their oldest customers can't tell which one of them is which. Maybe if both of them didn't have first names starting with "M." "They think he's the older one," said Mike with the type of brotherly teasing common in families with closely aged siblings.

They are not twins, but might as well be between sharing the same business, sharing the same last name, and having first names sounding similar enough to confuse people. But people know those names. The Fentons are established and they don't do a heck of a lot of advertising. Still, you can't give up on that altogether, so the show makes sense. "You still need to keep your name out there," Mike Fenton said.

The show also provides informational lectures about fishing and hunting in Alaska delivered by experts. Few people know the Kenai River better than

Robert Begich, Alaska Department of Fish and Game research biologist. Begich is based in Soldotna, where a large portion of the guides who work on the Lower River are based. It is pretty much ground zero during the king salmon fishing season, just for starters.

Begich gave a well-attended talk on fishing the Kenai River in a balcony of the arena. There were a lot of fundamentals covered, some basics too basic for veterans of the river. But there was a treasure trove of information for those who wanted to know more about various goings on than just sitting in a boat with the sun shining in their face as their line dangled overboard. Given Begich's level of expertise, fish studies, and time spent on the river, he was kind of like a fish whisperer and it behooved anyone who was going to spend some summer days on the Kenai to listen in.

The Kenai River drainage represents 25 percent of all the sportfishing in the state, Begich said. That is saying something since Alaska has a land area of 586,000 square miles, myriad lakes and creeks, and 6,600 miles of coastline, which is more than the rest of the United States combined. If islands are factored into that the total is about 34,000 miles. That is a heap of water. Although not every body of water has fish in it, I always wonder when I pass any lake or stream of any size if it does.

Begich noted that the Kenai is the largest rainbow fishery in the state, even if the river's reputation is more closely aligned with salmon. Begich did not talk about the fact that other salmon runs across the United States have crashed over the years. The Atlantic salmon took a major hit from overfishing between 1980 and 1990. Catch at sea from trawlers was blamed for much of the fish's demise. In recent years the Atlantic salmon has begun a slow comeback off the eastern US coast. Likewise, salmon populations in the Pacific Northwest were drastically affected by such things as dam building and overfishing and were classified as endangered.

The history of salmon populations elsewhere has led to numerous regulatory actions by Alaska's Department of Fish and Game with an eye to preserving the species. The department supervises a sonar counter that takes stock of fish entering the river.

"It's like a bank account," Begich said. "It estimates the passage of kings into the river."

Alaska authorities have established minimum escapement numbers for king salmon that must enter the Kenai River so that the fish won't be fished out. The goal is to keep kings running in perpetuity. If the kings do not seem to be returning in sufficient numbers to meet that goal action can be taken. Fishing can be halted altogether. Fishing with bait can be stopped. All fishing can be declared catch and release so no kings are removed from the river. A slot limit can be established prohibiting keeping fish of certain size, say forty-six to fifty-five inches, so those robust fish can live to fight again and grow into extra-large trophies. Those are all options in years of lean returns and at one time or another all of them have been invoked.

But it was only April and optimism ran high that it would be a good year for kings and that there would be no restrictions on fishing of any kind. There are five kinds of salmon, and Chinook, or kings, are the big ones, the most sought-after. Coho, or silvers, are far more plentiful. Reds, or sockeyes, are considered the tastiest by some and they come into the river by the hundreds of thousands or millions. Those species return from the ocean every year to spawn in the Kenai River. Pink salmon, or humpies, are on a two-year cycle, and return in even years. Chum salmon, or dog salmon, are not sought-after by anglers. Mushers who compete in the Iditarod Trail Sled Dog Race who have kennels loaded with huskies may feed chum salmon to their canines.

The Chinook, or king, is the sexy salmon. A "small" king salmon may weigh thirty-five pounds, yet that may be the biggest fish an angler ever catches in his life anywhere besides Alaska. The fisherman weaned on bass, perch, bluegill, walleye, or lake trout may consider a thirty-five-pound king to be a monster. By Kenai River standards it is a veritable pipsqueak. Typically, fishermen use twenty- or even thirty-pound test line to fish for kings. By comparison, catching those mini-fish in the Lower 48 might involve six-pound test. It's pretty much the difference between dental floss and a rodeo lasso.

"Big salmon," Begich said, "is one of the things the Kenai River is famous for. Sixty percent of the run averages forty pounds."

Ever since the world-record ninety-seven-and-one-quarter-pound king was caught in 1985 fantasies have run rampant that there is a bigger one out there waiting to be hooked. The one-hundred-pound king must exist, it is believed, and every guide and every knowledgeable fisherman wants to become a legend on the Kenai River.

In his own way, Dan Myers, a longtime Kenai guide, who was trying to drum up business at the Sportsman Show for Alaska Clearwater Sport Fishing, is already a river legend because of his up-close-and-personal encounter with a mammoth king. It was not the big one that got away, but the big one he refused to let get away. It was not the world record, but it was close enough to make a man do something daffy.

Myers is fifty-five now, but in 1985, just two months after the record was caught in May he was younger and perhaps more foolish. He has no trouble remembering the date, July 9. The record catch provoked a fever of sorts on the river that year. Everyone thought that if there was one gigantic fish out there, then there must be others lurking. Just had to be. Everyone knew it. Stood to reason.

Then, as now, Myers was a guide, though at the time he was employed by a company called Freebird Charters. That was his first season on the river after coming north from Loveland, Colorado. He went out fishing at 6 A.M., the regular time for starting a trip since under the state's regulations governing Kenai fishing for kings, guides can only circulate on the water between 6 A.M. and 6 P.M.

"We were out on the water for quite a while," Myers recalled. "It was nice out. I wanted to catch a big king."

Myers was accompanied by a man and his son. The client had caught two kings already, but let them go because they weren't big enough to suit him or be keepers. There was only one rod in the water as the boat nestled behind a big rock. Boom! Fish on!

A king salmon has exceptional reserves of strength it can put to use when it is scared and fighting for its life. If it is only lightly hooked it will spit the hook out and run free. If it is solidly hooked then the battle commences.

"It was a good fight," Myers said. "It pulled us back and forth across the river for twenty minutes."

Of course the king was underwater the entire time and neither the angler nor Myers could judge its size. It felt big, for sure, but there was no way to know just how big it was. How heavy a fish feels during the fight to reel it in may depend on its personality as much as its body type.

"You never know," Myers said. "I've had big fish come in like a wet rag and I've had thirty-pounders fight like hell."

The fish broke the surface and the men got their first look at the king. Still, it wasn't as if Myers then had the eye to judge size from a fleeting glance that he does now after so many years of experience. He knew this king was a keeper, but couldn't really guess its weight.

"It wasn't uncommon to catch sixty- to seventy-pound fish," he said. "I knew it was big. We didn't get too overly excited, but it was definitely a fish that he wanted."

Even the client recognized the difference between this baby and the ones he set free.

The fish was hooked solid. It wasn't going anywhere as long as they didn't botch the last steps reeling it up to the boat and coaxing it into the net. When a big fish is on and other boats are nearby, it is courtesy for their captains to rev up and get out of the way and for other fishermen to reel in. It is unpredictable what will happen when a beast of that size and strength is pulling. Myers looked up and his boat was about twenty feet from shore. He was in the front of the boat and the angler was in the rear.

After the arm-straining fight the fish was tiring and was coming in. When the resistance ceases that is a signal for the fishermen to crank the line for the last stretch and get that fish right up tight against the boat. It is the guide's job to net the fish.

"I put the net up and the fish was too big to fit into the net," Myers said.

That was a shocking moment. For the first time they recognized the fish was bigger than anyone thought and they also realized that standard operating procedure was not going to work.

"That fish was never going to fit into the net," Myers said. "Then the hook got caught on the netting when the fish had his head in it. I'm thinking, 'It ain't gonna go.'" Uh, oh.

This was a guide dilemma. The fish was still hooked, but it couldn't be captured in the net. It was a dynamic fish that had to be kept and weighed. What to do? "All looked dire," Myers recounted with a building level of drama in his voice. "It was an ugly situation. But it was a dandy fish."

The answer flashed through his mind. "I just jumped in the river," he said.

Myers was wearing waders, but only a T-shirt on his torso. Kenai River water, even in July, can be in the forties or fifties, though no one really pays attention because nobody goes in the water on purpose and nobody stays in it long enough to care if they do.

The river level was only a few feet high where Myers jumped in—up to the top of his waders. The water was cold enough to provide a little shock, but Myers was a man on a mission, wanting to make sure he hugged that fish so it didn't swim off over the horizon. At first the tide was pushing the fish right into him so it was easy to hang on to it. But a man has only two hands and Myers held the net in one hand and grabbed the fish in the other. He was still trying to use the net as a weapon in some way to his advantage.

After Myers took his plunge, nobody was steering the boat and it began drifting downstream. The boat and passengers floated away as Myers wrestled with the fish. The boat was not moving too fast, a few miles per hour, and he didn't think anything bad would happen

"I'm not worried about them so much as the fish," Myers said. "I'm still connected to the fish. It was a good thing we fought the fish to exhaustion. That was smart of us."

And more than a little helpful. The fish was out of energy, so Myers had the upper hand. As the boat began floating off he yelled, "Row to shore!"

Then he took his own advice, trying to walk to shore. "When my feet got on the ground I felt a little bit more comfortable," Myers said. "It was still a struggle. It was very awkward."

Eventually, the boat got to shore without casualties and Myers got to shore with the fish. Once he actually laid it out and admired it he was convinced it had to be weighed. They had something special, no doubt. The fish was still squirming around and Myers subdued it with a few hits to the head with a rock. He didn't want to hit it too hard, though, and make it bleed.

When a big fish is captured and weighing it is paramount, time is of the essence. Fish lose fluids when they die, so they get rushed to scales to be weighed ASAP. Myers was reunited with the boat and the other occupants were amazed by the size of the fish, which he laid down in the center of the flat-bottom boat for safekeeping. Myers wrapped the fish in a wet jacket to help prevent the fish from drying out.

"I have no doubt I saved a pound there," he said.

A single pound could have been a difference maker in a potential record challenge. Ounces may have made a difference. They had no way of estimating weight except in a general way. Next stop was Charlie's Tackle Shop, the closest place for a weigh-in. As it so happened, the tackle shop was running a contest for the heaviest fish weighed in that summer—first place was a free mount. Myers's man won.

The fish was not a world record, but it was within shouting distance. The official weigh-in registered the king at ninety-two and one-quarter pounds. Myers was pretty proud of that fish—still is.

"It was the biggest fish caught with a guide for about five years," he said. "It's the biggest fish caught out of a drift boat."

The basic theme of the comments made at the time to Myers for his overboard exploit was: "You're dedicated, buddy."

Some twenty-seven years had passed since Myers went for a swim in pursuit of the big fish, but his passion for the Kenai River has never waned.

"Oh, man, it's a special river," he said. "Each river's got its own draws, its own pluses and minuses, what people go there for. I haven't seen a river that's as diverse as the Kenai. It's prolific. It's a wonderful stream. A very fertile river—and pretty."

The world record has stood since 1985. Does Myers believe he will see a new record some day, something that tops ninety-seven and one-quarter? "I always want to stay optimistic," he said.

One thing Myers can answer with authority, though, if anyone ever asks— If the big one is on the hook and is about to get away, what would you do?

"I went in after it," he said.

Alaska Rivers Company rafting operator Gary Galbraith fits Malachi Willis, eleven, one of my grandsons, with a life jacket before rowing eleven miles down the Kenai River.

May

THE MAN WHO LOVED THE RIVER

The Kenai River stole Bob Penney's heart long ago and he has been trying to pay it back ever since.

A real estate man who could live anywhere, Penney chose the banks of the Kenai to build his dream house, if only used seasonally. The house was built on a low bluff overlooking the water and it was built not only for the convenience of his escape to his favorite slice of paradise, but as a retreat to host friends, to take them fishing.

It has long been said that if you want to catch big fish, go fishing with Bob Penney. He has both luck and knowledge, and evidence displayed on the walls of his home supports that thinking. The walls in the living room, small guest bedrooms, hallways, and bathrooms are covered with framed photographs of Penney relatives and associates who have caught king salmon in his company. There is picture after picture of people wearing smiles as wide as their faces as they struggle to hoist fish that weigh as much as a Labrador retriever. Fishing with Penney rubs off with good fortune.

In early May, Penney turned eighty. He is still tall and erect, trim with blue eyes, an energetic talker, and his thick sandy hair is still in place. A lifetime as a successful businessman

Bob Penney is perhaps the Kenai River's greatest protector. He was a major mover in founding the Kenai River Sportfishing Association and the Kenai River Classic, and he actively lobbies government officials for rules and regulations that would protect the river's habitat.

has earned him time to rest, but he seems congenitally unable to take it easy. His passion for the Kenai River remains as intense as ever. It is likely that no single person has done as much as Penney to help preserve the river's future.

Over recent years much energy has been focused on habitat preservation and restoration to prevent bank erosion. Penney was at the forefront of that movement. The Kenai River Classic was founded as a way to bring to the river influential politicians who deal with legislation that can affect it and as a fund-raising event. Penney was there at the beginning. The nonprofit Kenai River Sportfishing Association was created to promote and protect the river's charms. Penney was at the root of that.

Penney began working construction in Anchorage in 1951 when he was nineteen after moving north from Oregon, and eventually became a builder and real estate magnate. He is tight with Alaska political figures and that has sometimes made him a controversial figure on state issues. To commercial fishermen he is pretty much the bogeyman, the biggest lightning rod for criticism, the most visible individual supporter of sportfishing while they are trying to make a living catching the same salmon in nets.

Studies by the Sportfishing Association and other organizations, most recently in 2007, impart about a $1 billion value to sportfishing in Southcentral Alaska. There are no statistics solely for the Kenai River and the region involved includes such bodies of water as Deep Creek, the Anchor River, the Moose River, and other locations. But indeed money does ripple through the Alaska economy from fishermen. The Alaska Department of Fish and Game report indicates that $561 million is generated by Southcentral sportfishing from resident anglers and about $428 million is generated in the area by nonresident anglers for a $988.5 million impact. That includes fishermen's spending and tax revenue and the report said that 11,535 jobs in the region are attributable to fishing-related spending.

The region is vast, including the Anchorage area, Prince William Sound, Kodiak Island, and Cook Inlet. The Kenai River is part of that and was singled out for comment in the report: "The Kenai River . . . is an easy drive from Anchorage and is widely known among anglers as one of the world's foremost salmon rivers."

Penney's mantra is "Fish come first." What he means is that if salmon are at risk as indicated by a smaller-than-expected return to spawn, any measure taken to halt fishing, sport or commercial, for a short period or a lengthy one, is justified. What he doesn't want to see are regulations that allow commercial interests to catch fish when anglers are left out. He views the Kenai River as a magnificent resource, but is not foolish enough to believe that it is an inexhaustible one.

King salmon are present in finite numbers as part of the natural world. To Penney, scooping up trophy king salmon in a net is like "cutting down a redwood tree for firewood."

The picture windows in Penney's elaborate home offer panoramic views of the river as it flows past. Gazing out at the winding waters can be a mesmerizing experience as they bend around a wide stretch and straighten again rolling toward Cook Inlet.

"Those are all video screens," Penney said of the windows. "I can sit down and watch it."

Bob Penney's love affair with the Kenai River began in 1976. He had fished elsewhere in Alaska with his children for years, until they discovered the Kenai. On that trip Penney's son Henry caught a king salmon that so astonished them that Penney never wanted to drop a line in the water ever again anywhere else in pursuit of Chinooks. Bob's memory is a little fuzzy on the weight. The fish was either sixty-two pounds or sixty-eight pounds, depending on what time of day you ask him. The point being is that if you want to catch big king salmon, this—the Kenai River—was the place to be and he was fascinated by that.

"There is nothing like going fishing here and having the opportunity to hook a sixty- or seventy-pound king," Penney said. "I don't care who you are, it affects the rest of your life. They are such gorgeous creatures."

Penney likes to say that the ten largest king salmon ever caught on rod and reel all came from the Kenai River. Alaska Fish and Game maintains a list for its trophy king salmon program that recognizes fishermen for catching kings that weigh at least seventy-five pounds. It used to recognize kings caught that weighed at least fifty pounds, but so many were being registered, according to biologist Bob Piorkowski, that the requirement was changed.

"Every one weighed over ninety pounds," Penney said. "That's how I fell in love with the resource."

The Fish and Game program does not match Penney's top ten, but the top eight largest kings on the list weigh more than ninety pounds and there are three others in the eighty-nine-pound-plus area. Certainly not all big kings have been registered, so Penney's boast is close enough.

The state list of 754 king salmon recognized ranges from Les Anderson's ninety-seven-and-one-quarter-pound world record down to fifty pounds. Every one of them was caught on the Kenai River.

THE WORLD RECORD

King salmon weighing more than 100 pounds have been caught in nets by commercial fisherman. There is a claim of a 126-pounder in a fish trap dating to 1949. But the catch of the ninety-seven-and-one-quarter-pound, sport-angler, rod-and-reel nabbed official world-record salmon is well-documented and a replica is accessible for viewing. The 100-pound king is the holy grail for fishermen and this came the closest.

The legendary fish was caught on the morning of May 17, 1985, by a Soldotna fisherman named Les Anderson. At the time Anderson was part owner of the local Ford dealership in the community, only a few miles from the spot on the river where he hooked the big one using a spin-n'-glo and salmon eggs for bait. Anderson was fishing with friend Bud Lofstedt and once he hooked into the monster he needed some encouragement. The fish was caught at about 6:30 A.M. at Honeymoon Cove, one of the euphoniously named segments of the river, but led Anderson on a merry chase.

The power of the sleek, gray salmon pulled the small fishing boat all over the river. Anderson grasped the rod tightly and Lofstedt steered the boat carefully. The fish fought its way upstream. Anderson, who was sixty-eight at the time, fought to keep the fish on. At times the fish was steering the boat. The fish did not reveal itself, so it was unclear just how big it was, but when Anderson reeled it close to the boat and it was obvious it could not fit into the net, well, that was plenty of information about its size. Three different times Anderson cranked the fish up to the boat before Lofstedt declared it a hopeless task to bring the fish into the net to lift it out of the water.

Reeling and holding, Anderson did everything right, but it didn't matter: the fish wasn't coming up. So Lofstedt guided the boat to shore and in a winner-take-all move, Anderson hauled the salmon up on land to quell it. The chests belonging to both Anderson and the fish heaved for breath. Once the salmon was subdued it was carried into the boat and the men made a dash for a scale. It was worthy of the speed, they knew. Was it a record? They didn't know that.

At that time the world-record king salmon taken on a rod and reel was a ninety-three-pounder caught in 1977 in Southeast Alaska by a Juneau fisherman named Howard Rider.

Anderson and Lofstedt brought the fish to Echo Lake Lockers for a weigh-in. There are no secrets in a fishing town and although not much time had passed, enough whispering occurred so that the three of them—Les, Bud, and the fish—were greeted by about twenty onlookers. Weight was the essential statistic, but the fish's other measurements were gargantuan, as well. It was measured at fifty-eight-and-one-quarter inches in length and thirty-seven-and-one-quarter inches in girth. The fish was a fatso. So many photos were snapped of Anderson holding the fish that it looked as if he would never tire of hugging it.

That might well have been true since a certain amount of disbelief attaches itself to a catch like this and by holding tight Anderson could prove that this fish was the genuine article.

Interestingly enough, at the time Bob Penney was the president of the Kenai River Sportfishing Association and the local newspaper, the *Peninsula Clarion*, called him for comment. "He's a lucky, lucky guy," Penney said.

Anderson was not a man who tended to brag or to show off. He was more self-effacing. He seemed a little bit dazed by the entire experience, but he did note that up until then the largest king salmon he had caught weighed sixty-three pounds. Nothing to sneeze at, but AAA minors compared to this Major League catch. Wouldn't you know it, there was already one honking big salmon in the family. His wife had caught an eighty-five-pound king and occasionally lorded it over him. No more.

The catch made worldwide headlines and helped solidify the Kenai River reputation in the minds of anglers as a mythical place. It whetted appetites, too. If there was one, there had to be another, was the prevailing philosophy. This King Kong of fish couldn't be the only one. There had to be a ninety-eight-pounder swimming around, right? Or a ninety-nine-pounder? Or maybe, really that one-hundred-pounder that everyone fantasized about.

Maybe Anderson's record wouldn't even outlast the summer. Maybe he would be a short-lived record holder. Maybe. Or maybe not. The summer came and went. The 1980s came and went. The 1990s were coming to an end. Wherever Anderson went he was introduced as "The Man Who Caught The World-Record King Salmon." It was his new middle name. It was his new nickname. It eclipsed his real name. He was That guy. A certain type of fella would have eaten it up, milked the fame for all it was worth. Anderson didn't mind the notoriety, but he didn't revel in it. He accepted it, but didn't seek it out. It just was. He was associated with The Fish. They didn't write it that way, but everybody said it that way. The Fish.

As the years passed, Anderson became more closely identified with The Fish and less emotionally attached to it. It was kind of wearing him down always being talked about as if he and the salmon were twin brothers. A decade after the catch I spoke to him about the symbiotic relationship and he expressed two things. He was surprised no one had broken the record yet and he said he wouldn't mind if someone did break it, especially if it was another local, a fisherman from Soldotna or Kenai.

For some time, the fish mount was on display at the car dealership. Good idea. C'mon in and see the world-record king salmon and while you're here would you like to take a spin in the new model Ford Explorer? After a while the fish got a change of scenery, moved about a mile up the road to the Soldotna Visitors Center overlooking the river. You didn't need to come prowling around pretending like you were looking for a new car to see The Fish.

More years went by and the record still belonged to Les Anderson. In 2003, eighteen years after Anderson and Bud Lofstedt went fishing one May morning, Anderson passed away. As of the end of the 2012 Kenai River fishing season, nine more years had passed for a total of twenty-seven years since the king of kings was caught. The record still belongs to Anderson, posthumously.

Penney won't use the word superstition to describe how he spends his early mornings of each May 17, but what else can you call it? He makes sure he is out in his boat on the Kenai and that a thermos of coffee comes with him. At 6:30 A.M. Penney drinks a toast to Les Anderson, The Man Who Caught The World-Record King Salmon. And then he drops a line and hopes to beat the record.

THE BIG FISH ON DISPLAY

Whoever wants to see the record fish still can, anniversary date of its death or not. The mount is the feature display in the Soldotna Visitors Center and always, always the first thing noticed is the gosh-darn fish's girth. Sure, it is plenty long at nearly five feet, but its midsection, that's where the weight was. The fish looks as if it swallowed a basketball just before it swallowed Anderson's hook.

Periodically, every year or so when I'm in the area and passing by I make a pilgrimage to the fish. I don't do a Bob Penney and toast Les or the fish with a caffeinated beverage, but I do stare thoughtfully at the mount in its glass case. Big fish, I think. Big, damned fish.

On a May day, not the seventeenth, I stopped in to visit The Fish. It lives amidst many other fish and wildlife mounts, surrounded by tourism brochures. Robert Saari, the twenty-one-year-old lad minding the store, said in mid-July of 2009 when fishing with his grandfather and one of his granddad's friends in a flat-bottomed boat on the Kenai River not far from the community of Sterling he hooked an eighty-six-pound king.

"I don't know if I want to try again," said Saari, marveling at the power of the salmon. "It almost pulled me overboard. I literally saw my life flash before my eyes. That fish scared me."

The fight lasted about twenty minutes, but Saari said it felt more like an hour to his weary arm and shoulder muscles. He didn't think there was much chance he was going to land it without help, but he did. They toted the fish home and weighed it and grandpa thought Robert should have it mounted. He didn't.

"I ate it," he said. "It fed me, my brother and sister and parents for a good portion of the winter."

That was Saari's brush-with-greatness fish. Since then the biggest king he had landed was forty-nine pounds. As if to most of the known world a fish weighing that much wouldn't be impressive.

"It's not a dream fish, but it's a good-sized fish," he said.

The Visitors Center is housed in its own building on a main drag in Soldotna, but is only an informational destination, not a place that has shows or lectures that will pack in the fans. There's no doubt, though, that one reason people stop by is to take a gander at the world-record fish.

"Oh, every day people come in and ask about Les's fish," Saari said. "Every day, all day. How do they react? 'Wow, that's a big fish.' That's what they say. I don't know if I could have caught that fish."

When Saari's fishing grandfather learned that he was working at the Visitors Center he teased him a bit. "He said, 'You better take care of that fish.'"

And he does. When he unlocks the doors and turns on the lights in the morning he shrugs off his jacket and starts work. He gives the fish its due, immediately dusting the outside of the glass case that holds Les Anderson's fish.

"That's my first stop in the morning," Saari said.

Quality time with The Fish.

SPRING FISHING

Mid-May is often chilly on the Kenai River. You might get bright sun or you might get cold rain. Les Anderson imbued mid-May with magic, but as the years went on May attendance dropped off. People work. Kids go to school. Who wants to shiver on a boat for six hours? There was less competition on the river. Crowds were down.

Sometimes the water didn't even cooperate in May. During a particularly cold spring the glacial runoff was slow to make its way from the Kenai Mountains to the Kenai River and the water level ran low. The Kenai is not a deep river. Usually, when it is robust in most places it is not more than six feet deep. When the water level is at four feet fishermen can still put boats in, but big rocks, always submerged in summer, may be visible. Sandbars are closer to the surface. The unwary captain can steer his boat right into an entrenched boulder or over a gravel bar and turn his prop into confetti. Big repairs. Big bill.

Still, I liked the mid-May Kenai king fishing. The first run of kings might return around May 15, so you were taking one of the first shots at them. If the kings trickled into the river at a pace too slow to suit Fish and Game, however, there were times when rules were trotted out to hold down the catch. No bait, just bare, naked hooks, might be allowed as the weapon of choice. Or catch and release. Meaning anglers could catch a king, but couldn't keep it. It had to be set free after being reeled in.

Often enough (too often) I was skunked on these half-day excursions. But one year I got lucky and caught a king that didn't spit the hook, didn't laugh in my face, and nobly fought back as I reeled. Of course it was hooked during a catch and release span so I couldn't keep it and eat it.

There is an erroneous belief that there is twenty-four hours of daylight all over Alaska during the summer. If you travel to the Far North, to Barrow on the Arctic Ocean, or other small villages above the Arctic Circle, you will experience round-the-clock sunshine on and around June 21, the date of the summer solstice. But hundreds of miles to the south, in Anchorage and on the Kenai Peninsula, it never reaches the point of twenty-four-hour daylight. At its peak, there are about twenty-one-and-one-half hours of daylight in Southcentral.

That does mean when you go fishing in May at 6 A.M., it's already bright. With my work schedule, I went when I could go, even if a guide was discouraging because of the low fish count at the sonar and because of restrictive rules. Other anglers stayed away in droves, but I sometimes showed up when it was counterintuitive to believe it would be a good fishing day.

MY BIG FISH

One day more than twenty years ago I embarked on one of these foolish May errands, daring the odds. The birds were out, the trees were in bloom, and the sun was high in the sky, its rays beginning to warm what had been a borderline frost of a morning.

There are times when I think of the Kenai River area—and many areas of Alaska really—as a landscape painting come to life instead of the opposite, a man-made copy of real life on canvas. There is always solitude, peace, in my pictures, except when I am actually on the river and boat engines rev as they carry fishermen to the fish.

Generally speaking, Kenai River fishing boats are about twenty feet long. They have flat bottoms that draw very limited drafts. And they are open to the elements. No canopies. Most guides use basic variations and paint the name of their guide services on the sides.

In the 1980s, when there were reports of huge kings in the seventy-, eighty-, and even ninety-pound class being caught regularly, fishing on the

Kenai was almost out of control at times. On a sunny, summer Saturday there might be 500 boats on the Lower River with 2,000 fishermen hungry for the super king. It was a boom time for Alaska, everyone had money and the real estate market sizzled.

Then there was a housing market collapse (people tossed their keys to the bank as they exited the state), the economy was shakier than one of the many earthquakes that rattled the state, and the salmon seemed to go into sympathetic decline, too.

On the day I joined John Rudd of Fish Hawk Charters on a Tuesday morning, he said, "I'll be surprised if I see four boats." This was an eyebrow-raising comment because the Kenai River is closed to guide activity on Sundays and Mondays, to keep the pressure off the fish. So usually, Tuesday is a huge day, New York–subway system crowded. He was right, though. Over miles of river we saw about fifteen boats.

The lure of the Kenai River during the early season is giant king salmon. Fishermen want to catch them, measure them, heck, practically cuddle them the way Les Anderson did in his fish pictures. Then they want to mount them if they are big enough and take them home and eat them. Catch and release regulations can turn the Kenai into a ghost town, with hotel reservations cancelled, restaurants stuck with wide-open seating at dinnertime, and guides twiddling their thumbs on shore. Call me when the fish are back, is the cry of the angler.

There were fish in the river, just not enough to satisfy Fish and Game at that point in the run. I learned quickly that catch and release definitely weeded out a large number of fishermen not willing to pay $75 for a guided trip (the rate at the time). It would not be exactly accurate or fair to say that the rule placed a padlock on the river since a fisherman could still go out, but the scenario was a discouraging one.

As always, Bob Penney, who at that time was chairman of the Sportfishing Association's board of directors, had a trenchant observation about what he was witnessing. He was still in his summer home on the river and he still took his boat out for a little fishing a couple of days before I was out. Fishing in what past experience told him was normally a good place to catch a king, he not only didn't catch one, he didn't even see anyone else trying.

"There was not a rowboat, not a drift boat, not a powerboat," Penney said. "When there are fish to be caught, fishermen show up immediately, and when there aren't, there are no fishermen there. It's instant. It's unbelievable. The Kenai is so peaceful, so serene, and so sad."

Penney's slogan, motto, mantra is "Fish come first." That is the official policy of the state of Alaska, if not in those exact words. Salmon are born in the Kenai River, head out to sea, and after spending years in the ocean return to the Kenai River to spawn. They spawn and they die.

There are two runs of returning king salmon each year in the spring and the king fishing season extends pretty much from mid-May until July 30. The first is based on the fish showing up and the closure is by government fiat. After July 30 a fisherman cannot keep a king salmon. Although there are always other kinds of fish around, the actual king fishing season is a short one of roughly ten weeks.

Years ago, the state Board of Fisheries and Fish and Game approved and implemented policies based on fish counts the number of kings that came into the river from Cook Inlet. A minimum escapement number was chosen. In 1991, when I was fishing with Rudd, the rule said that if the state agency could not project a return of 5,300 king salmon for the first run, the fishery was closed.

It is interesting to review the potential reasons offered at the time for the low return. Trawler fleets intercepting kings in the Pacific Ocean while they were on their migration path back to the Kenai River was one. A mysterious disease was another thought floated. So was too much commercial fishing, as was an overfished sport fishery. They were all just theories, but whatever the reason the fish shortage meant that John Rudd and I were fishing in comparative solitude and even if I caught the world record to top Les Anderson, I couldn't keep it. I figured there was a better chance that I would be able to walk across the surface of the Atlantic Ocean from New York to London than best Anderson's record, so I wasn't too worried about the restriction.

Catch and release was viewed virtually as punishment by Alaskan fishermen who wanted their king salmon, yet the catch and release ethic has experienced a gradual growth in angler attitude in the Lower 48 if only because of the popularity of the BASS circuit. Catch and release was a cornerstone aspect of the southern bass fishing circuit promulgated by founder Ray Scott. That high-profile competition stressing catch and release, combined with the increase in fly fishing and its own emphasis on catch and release, expanded the focus in the United States.

In many areas a catch and kill approach has prevailed for decades and that was especially true in areas where catching panfish to feed the family and fill the freezer was a major element on dinner menus. That was an outlook totally different from sportfishing and tournament fishing.

Some might argue that the Alaska fisherman was spoiled in being able to travel a short distance to the Kenai River and either by their lonesome, or in cooperation with a guide, fish for the world's largest and tastiest king salmon. Suddenly being told by the government that they couldn't do so rankled the most independent minded of thinkers.

"What people want to see," said Rudd, "is the fish hanging on the scale and them in a picture standing next to it."

That's in an ideal world. It was no longer an ideal world, if only temporarily. If kings were plentiful in the second run, the restrictions would be lifted. But a fisherman could still have much of the same experience. We were surrounded by the beauty of the river. We could soak in the shore scenery. I fished and hoped a king salmon would bite.

Rudd's assistant guide actually thought that the action would be better than usual because of less competition from other fishermen. A few days earlier he had one fisherman out who hooked five kings in a morning.

As part of the always-in-place generally restrictive rules, a fisherman cannot keep more than one king salmon in a day anyway. Since he couldn't keep a king at all the man kept fishing, kept catching and releasing. My luck was not quite that good. But I caught a rainbow trout, released since the season wasn't yet open on them. I caught what passed for a miniature king that was estimated to weigh fifteen pounds. Capturing a fifteen-pound fish just about anywhere else in the rest of the country would be cause for celebration. On the Kenai such a fish would be released 99.9 percent of the time anyway because it wouldn't measure up—it just wouldn't be big enough to bother hanging on to.

Then it happened. I hooked a king that given its fight seemed more than run-of-the-mill. I cranked the reel, the fish resisted. I reeled, the fish pulled. Several minutes passed. I gained the upper hand slowly, but steadily. I could feel a strain in my arms as I attempted to keep the rod tip high and the slack tight. The fish was headed in now, straight to the boat. The fight had been exhausted out of it. Reeled right up to the boat, the fish went limp. It was a beauty. It was a big-un. To me, anyway. Rudd, a much bigger man than me, and with much larger biceps, lifted the fish into full view. He made quick calculations based on catching and studying between 5,000 and 6,000 kings.

The fish was out of the water only for a matter of seconds, but Rudd estimated its weight as forty-five pounds and its length as forty-eight inches.

"I can tell within two pounds," Rudd said. "Any guide can."

Leaning over the side of the boat Rudd dragged the fish back and forth in the water, trying to spark its revival. It worked. Rejuvenated, the fish shuddered into action and then swam away. Released. I had my look at it. The fish was long, heck four feet long is something to behold. It was as heavy as a school-aged kid. The color, the silver sheen, is what stayed with me. Under ordinary circumstances the fish was definitely a keeper, a catch to be proud of. Carving it into salmon steaks for future meals would have been nice, but I was OK with seeing it swim off and disappear, too. I knew I caught it. Trusting Rudd's analysis, I knew how big it was.

Would I have preferred to take salmon home? Yep. But it was a great day anyway. Part of that was the river. Just being out on the Kenai River on a sunny day is a worthwhile outdoor experience, a chance to appreciate nature. Catching king salmon may be the goal, but it doesn't have to be the end all.

That was a long time ago and that king salmon is still the biggest one on my resume. I had a fiberglass mount of that fish made based on Rudd's mathematical estimates. To me the only thing I missed out on was the meat. Since I have gone oh-for-the-day in pursuit of kings many times I'd have to say that I rate this catch and release trip as far superior to others. It was akin to living the phrase "better to have loved and lost rather than never to have loved at all."

Two decades later I still have the mount, but it is not in an honored position on a wall at the moment. It has been in the past, but there is some marital opposition involved. Seizing the right moment, however, I am confident it will make a comeback.

MAY FEELS LIKE WINTER

As Les Anderson learned, May on the Kenai can be generous. It's unpredictable. May of 2012 was not one of those years, though. Record snowfall in Southcentral Alaska meant that the snow cover in the mountains was slow to melt and the water level on the river was unseasonably low.

Bob Penney was back for the summer, but he wasn't ready to go fishing because he was ill and the river wasn't ready to have him. Kings were slow to return, too. The situation was a perfect storm of bad karma in early May. That didn't mean the Kenai wasn't on Penney's mind—and it was right outside his front door. He is always uneasy when something interferes with the opportunity to catch king salmon, whether it is Mother Nature, other humans, or the unknown.

Penney converted from a passionate fisherman, starting in 1977, to a proselytizing fisherman by 1984, when the Kenai River Sportfishing Association was created, heavily relying on $45,000 he used to jump-start the organization. Penney sought equal rights in the division of salmon in the river between commercial fishermen and sportfishermen and worried that commercial fishermen, the permit holders who make their living by capturing net-loads of fish, would dry up the resource through overfishing.

"My number one goal is to provide opportunity for the public to have a right to fish the Kenai River," Penney said. "We have as much right to those fish as anybody. One of my thoughts is that my grandson has a right to sportfish. He should be allowed that opportunity to catch fish. A commercial fisherman has the right to commercial fish. It's a paradise to me. It's probably become the biggest single cause for me to preserve it for my grandchildren."

It was Penney's idea to preserve fish for the future by preserving the salmon's spawning grounds. There had been much angst about bank erosion, the water lapping at the shore and shrinking the land. It was close to shore where salmon returned to spawn, so if the beds were eroded, the salmon, very much creatures of habit, might be stressed and become disoriented. If the salmon didn't spawn in the river, eventually there would be no more salmon in the river.

Habitat preservation and conservation became the chief cause of the Kenai River Sportfishing Association. Conservation began at home. Penney beefed up the shoreline of his property. He advocated for spending to spruce up and build buffers for the shoreline on state land. Others with riverfront property saw the wisdom and they took action to add protective rocks, tires, fencing, a variety of things, to the banks at the edge of their property. Where erosion control on other rivers was not as widely embraced, the fisheries took a hit.

There was no such thing as conservation in the United States until Teddy Roosevelt became president. He was essentially the first environmentalist with clout. The environment throughout the United States has many powerful advocates these days, but it is a never-ending battle on myriad fronts and those advocates are needed from the White House to the state house to the local town council.

Fish come first is Penney's motto, but in practical terms different steps could be taken to prove it.

"There's a fishing opportunity because if we didn't take care of the habitat—we've learned the hard way—there wouldn't be any fish," Penney said. "Look at all of the streams down south (in the Lower 48) where fisheries have disappeared. I think 75 percent of the reason they disappear is because habitat was destroyed. They took farm pastures right out to the edge of the creek. They did everything they could to use all of the land and all of the habitat and the brush is gone. The biggest thing we've learned, I've learned, is how critical and important the habitat and the area where the fish live and spawn has to be protected. That's job number one."

There is no doubt that over the last decade habitat preservation consciousness adjacent to the Kenai River has multiplied tenfold, hugely.

"We learned that people didn't destroy the bank by walking on it intentionally," Penney said. "We didn't realize if you walked along that bank and made a path, the next spring the whole edge of that slope, that six-foot ball of grass, would be gone and the river could wash away the habitat. The habitat was gone. The public education thing was to tell people don't walk down the bank."

Anchorage newspapers—twenty years ago there were two of them—ran picture spreads and series describing the bank erosion. Penney said that was shock treatment for the public and the Sportfishing Association began lobbying the Board of Fisheries to make changes and to help awareness. A key was property owners taking charge of their own lands, buffering the end of their land at the river.

Habitat preservation and conservation is not a battle won overnight. It is an ongoing battle. Sometimes the river is going to be unruly and overflow its banks and there is nothing anyone can do about that. Humans can only do the best they can do. But these days as fishermen traverse the river they can gaze at wide swaths of property that are protected much better than they used to be. Just cruising past in a boat one can see it, one can tell. So much has been done to halt bank erosion. It is that obvious and that visible.

Ricky Gease is the executive director of the Kenai River Sportfishing Association based in Soldotna.

A few years ago the Pacific Coastal Salmon Recovery Fund invested $125,000 of money appropriated by Congress to study the effects of bank restoration on the Kenai River over a fifty-mile stretch between the mouth of the river and Skilak Lake. An environmental engineering company from Oregon performed the work and returned a thumbs-up verdict about the effects of restoration projects. A representative of the company said "the sheer density" of the Kenai projects was greater than those on any other river the firm had studied and that other areas could learn from what was being done on the Kenai.

While individual property owners committed to doing work on their own land, and many used their own dollars, they and others also were able to receive assistance from Fish and Game and the US Fish and Wildlife Service. This was essentially Penney's goal come to life.

And speaking of life, Ricky Gease, the current executive director of the Kenai River Sportfishing Association, coined the phrase that the river, due to the habitat restoration, was "being loved to life," instead of being loved to death as it might well have been at one time.

THE GUIDING LIFE

From his vantage point overlooking the river in his small office at the Harry Gaines fish camp, owner Reuben Hanke said the low water, coupled with late-season freeze-ups, made it impossible to launch a boat well past the normal mid-May start-up time. May 17, the Anderson day, came and went. May 20, no dice. May 25, uh-uh. It didn't matter how many king salmon were in the river if you couldn't fish at all. Forget catch and release, it was not possible to even try for kings if the boats were landlocked.

"I couldn't get a boat in through the ice at my boat launch," Reuben said. "We used to slip boats in the last few days of April or the first few days of May."

In an informal competition the guides used to brag about who could catch a king the earliest in the season. Reuben once caught a king on May 4. He remembers about ten years ago a guy catching a king on April 28. Not in 2012. Reuben did not launch his first boat of the season until May 29. Much before that and he would have had to use a Russian icebreaker and an augur to fish. It was kind of the reverse of global warming on the Kenai.

Typically, it is Alaskans who fish in May. Tourists don't start visiting until a bit later in the season. Those would-be Alaskans who had the fishing fever and didn't want to wait longer. Catching a king was possible, but far from guaranteed. "We never caught kings consistently in early May," Reuben said. "But this is just ridiculous. It was just a tough winter."

When Reuben says it was a tough winter that's a longtime Alaskan speaking. It's not some cheechako newcomer who just showed up from Florida for his first winter in the north. For a month after Christmas the temperature in Soldotna hit subzero regularly and even dropped to minus thirty.

The dastardly winter contributed to the late start to fishing. On a heavy snow year like this one, when the melt comes, it rushes into the river and it is usually dirty water. The muddy nature makes it difficult for fish to see and if fish can't see they are not going to respond to colored lures. They'll swim right by them without a glance.

At times when the water is high and the snowmelt sweeps down from on high, gathering tree branches and debris logjams form and the river floods. Reuben had knee-deep water in his yard that spring. That stuff happens from time to time. The Kenai is a river and it is wild. I always say that if you live along a river sooner or later it is going to get you with flooding and periodically the Kenai proves the point. If you live on a lake you probably won't have the same hassle.

Reuben, who is fifty-three, has lived along the river for more than twenty-five years and he has the same regard and love for the Kenai as Penney does. He's a lifer, but he doesn't really know what that is defined as. He thinks that means he will guide as long as he is able. "I don't know when I'm gonna quit. I'll quit when I can't do it anymore."

He looks at you like you must be a little bit touched to even ask why, but if you probe, Reuben says, "It's the Kenai" in such a manner of all-knowingness like no other explanation should be necessary. It's the same answer mountaineers give when asked why they climb the highest mountain in the world. "Because it is Everest," they say.

"In salmon circles, people know what that [the Kenai River] is," Reuben said. "People all over the world dream of catching salmon here."

Those fisherman from all over the world understand that the world-record king salmon was caught on the Kenai River, but the funny thing is, Reuben thinks, is that they don't really know how big *big* is. Numbers are one thing. Wrenching a fighting king salmon out of the water with all of your might is an exercise difficult to duplicate.

There is a photograph in Reuben's booking office of Harry Gaines, the founder of the business, and our old friend holding a king-sized king. I have seen the photo hundreds of times and it has been reproduced on postcards used as advertising for Gaines's guide service, so I even have copies. "That thing lives forever," Reuben said.

In the picture Gaines is hoisting a gigantic salmon out of the water and smiling his impish grin for the photog. I don't even know if Harry could have lifted such a fish without giving himself a hernia, but the fish isn't real, it's a mount.

The biggest king Gaines ever caught as a guide weighed seventy-two pounds, Reuben said. The biggest king he ever caught as a guide weighed eighty-two pounds. It was fifteen to eighteen years ago, Reuben said, and the client was from Woodinville, Washington. The man planned to mount it and made a deposit with a taxidermist, but he later called back and cancelled the order because his wife got on his case and complained about the cost.

Reuben Hanke is a longtime guide on the Kenai River and operates the Harry Gaines Kenai River Fishing service. He loans his property for use as the fishing headquarters for the Kenai River Classic, the Kenai River Women's Classic, and the Junior Classic for kids.

Reuben grew up in Iowa, went to college in Wyoming, and was always fixated on a career in the outdoors. When he found Alaska, he never left. He has thick, brown hair that has been known to be carved into a mullet, a thick mustache, stands around six feet tall and has a sturdy build. As a fishing guide, hunter, and trapper, Reuben is in some ways the most Alaskan of all Alaskan men I've ever known.

When he showed up on the Kenai River in the 1980s, though, he was a beginning guide, working for one of Gaines's competitors. Gaines was one of a coterie of pioneer guides on the Kenai and also eventually acquired the nickname "Quarter Mile Harry" for an almost mystical ability to catch king salmon within a quarter of a mile of his fish camp. That was the rumor, anyway.

But every time Reuben passed Gaines sitting in a boat with his clients all of them were still fishing, indicating none had caught a fish. With a one-a-day king limit that meant everyone was getting skunked. Yet Harry had a reputation for anglers catching fish with him. Reuben got suspicious so he set himself up in a little perch at Poachers Cove nearby and spied on Gaines and his boat through binoculars.

It turned out that as soon as other boats were out of sight the fisherman who had already caught their salmon took their rods out of the water.

"He had all four fish," Reuben said. "He just didn't want anybody else fishing there. What a fricking genius." So Reuben called Gaines and paid him a visit at the fish camp in the old trailer he lived in (nothing like the structures Reuben has since built) and told him, "I'm on to you." Harry said that Reuben was a pretty sharp fellow for figuring things out and then said, "You want a job?" So Reuben went to work for Gaines in 1986.

"It was the best thing that ever happened to me," Reuben said. "Working with Harry was like nothing else I ever did."

It turned out that if you worked for Harry and if you were friends with Harry that you had to be on guard all of the time for his practical jokes. Once, Harry removed the prop from the back of Reuben's boat so when it was time to go fishing the boat wouldn't go anywhere.

"He got me a lot," Reuben said. "But I got some payback."

Like the time Harry was using the outhouse and Reuben moved a car in front of the door. Reuben left him inside for forty-five minutes while he cussed and screamed.

"He finally settled down," Reuben said.

Harry had a longtime sponsorship deal with Coca-Cola. One of his boats was painted Coca-Cola red and white with the name of the soft drink on the side. Clients drank Coke products when they got thirsty out on the river. He had a Coke machine at the fish camp. One day Reuben quietly got into the Coke machine and replaced all of the cans of Coke with cans of Pepsi. There was a big crowd, maybe forty people who were fishing that day, when Harry went after a drink. When the can came down the chute as Pepsi, he was shocked. He went crazy and threw the can away.

Harry had a distinctive look. He had a snow-white beard that made him resemble Santa Claus (and he played the role locally at Christmastime) and always wore sunglasses. One time Reuben and three other guides pulled up right behind Harry's boat loaded with clients and all of the guides were decked out as Harry, wearing white beards and sunglasses. No one laughed harder at the gag than Harry.

When Harry died in 1991 Reuben was running the business. The majority of Kenai River fishing guides who own guide services place their names in the title of the business or on their boats. It would have been logical as one of the newer guys on the river for Reuben to have done so. But he never considered replacing Harry's name with his own. For a time that might have been valuable because Harry was a legend of the river, but more than twenty years have gone by and now, except among old-timers, Reuben Hanke is far better known today than Harry Gaines.

It was pretty much a matter of honor and loyalty for Reuben that he stuck with Harry Gaines Kenai River Fishing instead of making a change.

"There was no reason to do it," Reuben said. "Harry was a really good friend of mine. A guy who did the things he did, why would you want to change? Who was Reuben Hanke? I would never have dreamed of changing it. I hope it stays that way for thirty years."

There are no guarantees that Reuben and his wife, Kelly, will be running the guide service in thirty years, but there are no guarantees that one of their children, Ace, Chad, Jared, Beau, or Rachel, who is the youngest at twenty, won't be. The boys are scattered, but Rachel is around and she has decided she wants to become guide certified as soon as she can.

Reuben tells a story about Rachel when she was seven years old. She hooked a salmon from the bank, almost always a losing proposition given the way they run, and he stumbled upon her in the midst of an epic fight. She was pulling on the rod, facing away from the river, the pole over her shoulder trying to land that sucker. With that kind of determination in the blood, you never know. Maybe she is the born fisherwoman in the clan.

FINALLY ON THE WATER

The Harry Gaines fish camp has been greatly upgraded by Reuben over the years. He has built three on-premises, rustic, atmosphery cabins on a large deck to house anglers the night before they go out to fish. They can roll out of bed at 5:30 A.M. and stagger into the fishing boat that is docked perhaps forty yards from the front door.

There are durable plastic chairs to recline in and watch the river roll past as the sun sets. It is quiet, peaceful, and even if it is a bit gray and overcast (please don't let it rain in the morning, is the anglers' refrain) and in the low forties, it is still quite cozy. Inside the cabin the heat comes on. Yes, it is cold enough here in Alaska at the end of May, beyond Memorial Day, that you can still shiver in the night. In the rest of the country the temperatures are in the nineties, plus humidity.

A grassy patch stretches between the deck and the river. Directly across the water is a very steep, very high, seriously eroded bank, with houses set back from the cliff. A slight breeze rippled the trees. The wind picked up a little bit and some of the slighter trees swayed. This is still wild territory. A city is only five miles away, but right here there are the handful of buildings and the river. Over the doorway to Reuben's office are moose antlers. This is moose territory. One could walk by any minute, wade the river, or appear in the distance on the other side.

For a moment I recalled that for more than a quarter century I had been coming here, to this marvelous, dreamlike spot on the Kenai River for a day or two at a time. There have been changes on the property—it's grown up a bit. There have been changes on the far bank—it has shrunk a bit. But the river is the same. That's what really matters.

It was light at 5:30 A.M. when I awoke, ready to fish. The temperature was thirty-one degrees on the last day of May. That was the reading, but it didn't feel as cold on my skin as I thought it might. From shore I glimpsed a king salmon rolling, only a small part of its body visible above the surface. Was that a good omen?

Reuben was at the helm and I was fishing with Ricky Gease from the Sportfishing Association. Reuben's flat-bottom boat was powered by a fifty-horsepower Yamaha. I wore several layers for warmth, from a T-shirt to a shirt to a sweatshirt to a windbreaker. It was enough except for when we created our own windchill. That happened when Reuben opened the throttle, taking us downriver to find an advantageous place to fish. The water was shallow.

"I want to get by the rocks and sandbars," he said. "There aren't a lot of places you can run."

Some salmon hug the shore. Some congregate behind rocks. When they're moving upstream they generally stay away from the middle of the river. Reuben was trying to identify likely corridors that the fish—if there were any around—would take. After so many years invested on the Kenai, Reuben knows its contours well. That is part of a guide's education, understanding where the fish are likely to go. We can't see a thing in the water, even when the river is at its clearest, and it wasn't right then.

"When I was young I used to run all over the place," Reuben said, "and all that time your lines aren't in the water." He settled into a spot 16.5 miles upriver from Cook Inlet and told us to let our lines out a certain distance. At some point in their journey upstream the salmon would pass this spot.

"Whether they're biters or not, that's a whole different story," he said.

There were not many other boats in sight, wherever we moved, either guide boats, or private fishermen. It just wasn't crowded on the river. You could look at that as being to our advantage in that any fish available would be available to us. Or maybe we were just the most optimistic people in the whole area, ignoring the substandard return of kings in favor of believing if we just tried we would succeed. It was apparent that there were not many others like us with the same type of faith in a guide. Guides could operate from 6 A.M. to 6 P.M., but we were out for a half day, probably until 1:30 P.M. The returns were low so the catch and release rules had kicked in. Also, we could only use single hooks (no treble hooks) and no bait. A thirty-pound test line was attached to the Shimano rod. The technique was to bounce the hook on the bottom and hope a king salmon was attracted to it.

We had been out for a while when Gease was interrupted mid-sentence by a fish grabbing his hook. Fish on. He stood up and began reeling. Closer and closer it came. Then the fish did a smart thing. It dashed under the boat and in the process spit the hook and escaped.

Reuben looked at Ricky and said, "Oh, well, it was a bite."

I never saw the fish. Ricky never saw it well. Reuben guessed it was a twenty- to twenty-five-pound king, nothing spectacular, but a king nonetheless.

"That's when it happens," Reuben said of Ricky being caught in mid-discussion. "When you least expect it."

Gease has caught bigger. Much bigger. About five years ago he was out on the Kenai, three people in a boat, at another popular fishing hole called Sunken Island. He hooked and landed a seventy-four-pound, fifty-two-inch king salmon that came in after a twenty-minute battle. This one did not get away.

"It was a big fish and I knew it right away," Gease said. "People in other boats were getting out of the way. The fish led us all around. It was a good fight."

The fish went home with him and fed Gease, his wife, and visitors many a meal. "We ate it," he said. "Nothing better than fresh king." But they also canned quite a bit, cases worth.

Given his job at the Sportfishing Association, which he has held since 2004, Gease said people think he goes fishing all of the time. He actually has a desk job that involves a lot of paperwork, staying on top of legislative issues, studying government reports. He probably fishes for king salmon four or five times a year and for coho, or silver salmon, another couple of times. His job description does not call for catching fish, but making sure there are fish to be caught. Fisheries management is how Gease describes his task.

"Far from it," he said of him fishing all of the time. "We're doing work so other people can go out fishing all of the time."

Gease is from Racine, Wisconsin, and he fished a lot when he was a kid. He attended Stanford University and earned two degrees, a B.A. and an M.A. in biology and became a public school science teacher. When he tired of that he worked in outdoor education in Maine and twenty years ago moved to Alaska where initially he worked as a park ranger at the Kenai Fjords National Park near Seward, Alaska, also on the Kenai Peninsula.

If you stop by his office, one block off the Kenai Spur road connecting Soldotna to Kenai eleven miles away, he can print out reams of paper, reports of all kinds that catalog fish runs compiled by the state and economic impact studies that show how important sportfishing is financially to the Kenai Peninsula.

That morning, neither Ricky nor I made much of a contribution to either the sportfishing harvest or the lore of the river. Gease's one brush with a king was as close as we got to catching one to release. I never had a bite. As far as I was concerned the king salmon were a rumor. Or, as the Fish and Game sonar counter was telling everyone, there just weren't many king salmon around to catch. We hoped that would be a temporary condition and that as the weather warmed and the snowmelt ceased, kings would rush upriver from Cook Inlet.

No fish were caught by our boat despite the many, many years of expertise represented. "Any guide can take people out and catch them a fish," Reuben said, "but it takes a hell of a guide to go out for five-and-a-half hours and steer around them all day."

We accomplished that mission. Harry Gaines used to make fun of my inability to catch kings with him and I could imagine what he would say to sum up the half-day on the river. "Typical," I could hear him ribbing me. "You've got the whole river to yourself and you still couldn't catch a fish."

Motoring back to the fish camp without a king was not terribly troubling this time, however. We knew going into the day that the kings were not likely to be bountiful, so it was not an especially big surprise that we struck out.

I wasn't worried too much, either. This was going to be my year to top that 1991 forty-five-pound king. My season on the river was just starting and I should have more opportunities than I had ever had before to catch kings in one season. My turn was coming for sure.

For now, Les Anderson's legacy was safe from me—but not from Bob Penney. At least unofficially. Sitting in the Penney living room talking about fish, a favorite Penney pastime, talk turned to a monster-sized mount above his stone fireplace. The fish was red and it came with a story. Penney's narration went this way. Some years ago an angler caught the humongous sixty-inch fish and the claim was that it weighed 107 pounds. If so, that would have been a new world record.

The man brought it to a taxidermist for mounting and left it at the shop. There was only one problem. The fisherman caught it one day after the king salmon season closed on the Kenai River. He couldn't publicize his catch without incurring the wrath of authorities, without potentially facing legal charges and having the fish confiscated. So he abandoned the fish at the taxidermist's, disappeared, and eventually the fish came into Penney's possession.

There, by golly, according to Penney, hangs the world-record king salmon that nobody knows about and that isn't officially the world record. It is a hell of a conversation piece and to Penney it is a constant reminder that just maybe there is another king out there swimming in the river bigger than the one Les Anderson caught that long-ago day in May.

June

IT SEEMS TO BE RAINING RAINBOW TROUT

Kevin Thurman talks lovingly about rainbow trout, though often in shorthand. As in "you should have seen the 'bow we caught here." Or there. Or there. I have joined him on the cataraft on the Middle River, along with a friend of his, Lyman Meacham.

Elsewhere on the Kenai River the focus is on king salmon. It should be the heart of the run, and it being a Saturday, too, there should have been dozens, if not a couple of hundred boats on the Lower River. But that's not how it was on this mid-June day. King salmon have remained scarce and Fish and Game shut down king salmon fishing altogether, alarmed by the lack of blips from the sonar counter at what should have been the peak of the run.

The three of us were in a different world. We were only about twenty miles or so upriver from the king salmon territory, but we might as well have been on Mars for as many other fishermen we saw. It was cloudy and thirty-nine degrees when we pushed off from Bings Landing, a public boat launch between Soldotna and Sterling off the Sterling Highway. Our target was rainbow trout, but the offerings could include Dolly Varden, or possibly some sockeye salmon, or reds.

I had been looking forward to this trip since I met Kevin at the Sportsman Show in April and listened to him talk about the wonders of the Middle River. While king salmon are the most heavily publicized species that fishermen seek on the Kenai River, the rainbow trout fishery is probably its equal.

Rainbow trout are actually members of what is called the salmonid family. Compared to many other types of fish, they are rare throughout the United States, basically located only in the West. In some states they are considered endangered. No other place in the country has the concentration of rainbows to match Alaska.

A favorite of fly fishermen in Montana, rainbows get their name from their often spectacular coloration—pink, yellow, orange speckles on a silver body. They are noted more for length than weight and have accrued a certain status on the coveted fish meter. Perhaps because they are not seen in the East, South, or Southwest, rainbow trout have taken on a kind of mystique. In the movie *A River Runs Through It* rainbow trout are pretty much the only fish Brad Pitt, his brother, and his father care about. Like salmon, rainbow trout is a popular eating fish. Rainbow trout can be challenging to catch, rarely are caught in abundance, and many regulations exist to protect the species. An angler can only keep one rainbow trout in a day on the Kenai River.

The one a day is for eating. With nowhere convenient to cook and no one handy to share it with, I wasn't planning to keep a single one. Some people aren't interested in fishing if they aren't taking fish home for the freezer. Others—and I am one—love to catch fish, but if we can't take them home for some reason that's fine. The outdoor experience in nature, in the wilderness, being out on the water, the act of catching fish, is what it's all about to me and keeping the fish, especially in the case of a king salmon or rainbow trout, is a bonus.

Kevin's cataraft, its orange floats held together with wooden floorboards, was stable, but water splashed over the sides at times, so wearing waders with the feet attached like footie pajamas was mandatory if you wanted to stay dry. We proceeded on the water at a stately pace, no hurry, passing the cedar and log homes that real devotees of the river built, for the most part spaced reasonably far apart by dense stands of trees. In the few places where houses, mostly getaway cabins or seasonal homes, were clustered, the setting resembled a resort in Wisconsin. But we also came upon areas where it was just us and the woods.

Above all, if we stopped talking and spent our time looking, the water was spellbinding, the Kenai grayish in color today under the somewhat gloomy sky, but always moving, always hiding secrets. It was the water that led men to build those houses. It was the water that made men fall in love with the area. They want a piece of it. You can't own the river, but you can own the land that borders it, that will put you so close to the water you feel able to reach out and touch it from your yard, and in some cases can.

Unlike most bodies of water in Alaska, unlike many of the state's great fisheries, the Kenai River is located in a fairly densely populated area, running right through cities like Soldotna (population 4,163) and Kenai (population 7,945) and with roads constructed to fit its contours. Roads do not follow the entire river. Not hardly. But they make the river accessible in a way that no other phenomenal fishery is. The nearness of civilization to wilderness, the overlap even, is what makes dreamers out of people who feel they can afford a slice of paradise. The rest of us, the fishermen who come on day trips, are borrowers, not property owners, not residents.

We were freezing. "It's the middle of June and you've got to have gloves," said Lyman, sixty-seven, an Anchorage plumbing inspector who did not bring any. Not to worry. Thurman had extras in his supply cache aboard. I looked at Lyman and said, "That's why they call it Alaska."

It was Kevin's bare skin that I wondered about. He stood at the console wrapped in a hooded sweatshirt, acting impervious to the wind blowing in his face when we zipped along instead of floating. The cataraft could go about twenty miles per hour and when we went that fast it meant we were fighting the chill. That was a big part of the explanation for why we were so cold. Of course we wore layers, sweatshirts, jackets, and the like over the basic clothing, and the waders provided extra warmth. We also wore lifejackets over our layers. No way I could bend forward and touch my toes with all of that stuff on. But from a weather standpoint, when we sat still to fish we were fine.

Thurman pointed toward a tree to highlight an eagle's nest. Darned if a second or two later I saw an eagle. Bald eagles are plentiful along the Kenai River, and not a day had gone by on the river yet when I hadn't seen at least one from a distance, either flying overhead or perched on a tree branch. The white head was a giveaway, recognizing even from afar that it was the majestic bird in our line of sight. This one eschewed trees and sat on a rock, its eyes watchful as we floated on the water. The eagle was very stern looking. In a human the expression would be described as grumpy, perhaps attached to the thought, "What are you doing here?"

We had the same reaction when we saw a moose trotting through someone's backyard. Moose are common on the Kenai Peninsula. Moose-car collisions are so frequent that government agencies keep track and post signs announcing the count of moose fatalities. Not mentioned on the signs is the number of auto fatalities. Moose can weigh 1,200 pounds, aren't frightened by approaching automobiles, and from the force of the impact, the car usually crumples.

One time out fishing on the river, a mama moose with calf was trying to swim across to the other side and after splashing along for a few minutes the two of them surfaced right at the cataraft. At first Thurman and his client were wary. Then they whipped out the cameras and got terrific moose close-ups.

"Man, what a beautiful day," Thurman said, applying a different standard than the usual to the weather. "You don't want too much sun. It'll spook the fish. When it's like this they'll bite all day." So I was supposed to be happy for the grayness in the sky.

Still heading north we crossed the boundary into the Kenai National Wildlife Refuge. Not all of the Kenai River is in the refuge, only sections of it. The refuge consists of 1.92 million acres and is home not only to those pesky moose, but brown bears in abundance, black bears, too, trumpeter swans, and numerous kinds of migratory birds in addition to those eagles.

"This is nice up here," Thurman said, nodding toward the river's glassy surface. "This is rainbow alley. I have hundreds of hours in here. This is super to be right here."

Why super? Here Thurman caught a thirty-inch rainbow trout with an eighteen-inch girth, a trophy-sized fish. Rainbows of that length are hard to find in spring and summer, but not in early October when the second run of rainbow trout hit the Kenai. At that time of year big rainbows become common and tantalize fishermen.

Thurman built the cataraft on his own. When Meacham and I began fishing we threw flash flies and leeches into the water on balsa wood floats. Thurman tied all of them. "It gives him something to do in the winter,"

Meacham said. Yes, it does. Thurman ties hundreds of flies in the off-season, he said.

Lyman pointed as some rainbows jumped out of the water. We were in a channel with a gravel bar and the water was shallow on both sides of us.

"We're taking our time," Thurman said. "We're not in a hurry. We're finesse fishing."

Fish hit when you aren't ready. One minute you are talking and the next the rod is bending and a fish is hooked and running. I was turning my head to speak when the first fish hit the rod. I reeled and there was our first rainbow of the morning. Brightly colored, it was only about twelve inches long, but it occasioned comment. "Nice little 'bow," Thurman said as he released it.

Swiftly, there was another bite. This fish hit hard, but with subtlety, confusing me as to just what it was. "Play the fish so it doesn't spit the hook," Thurman ordered. Moments later it was in the net and seconds after that the thirteen-inch rainbow was released. "That one had the same nice color," Lyman said.

It was good to be reminded early that there were actually fish in the river, but the ones reeled in while beautiful in appearance could have been larger. "There are some big boys out there," Thurman promised.

"With our name on them," I said. "With your name on them," he said. "I'm not fishing today. I'm fishing through you."

Lyman hooked a fish and brought it to the boat, though it wasn't very big. "I've got the prize for the smallest one," he said. "I'm waiting for that big one."

The next strike was a powerful hit and I could tell right away the fish was stronger than the others. But a minute later it escaped after twice leaping out of the water into the air a few inches above the surface. "That was a big fish, man," Thurman said. "The whole key is you've gotta keep the pressure on the whole time."

It was touch. Reel when the fish relaxed, go slack when the fish ran. Put the pressure on the fish to swim in our direction, toward the boat.

The sky was clearing. The sun burst through the clouds. In the distance we could see snow-covered mountains. Lyman had a fish on. Hovering nearby was an eagle that looked mighty interested in the proceedings, as if contemplating a dive at it the next time the trout jumped. The eagle controlled its instincts. "That would have been pretty neat," Meacham said.

Several hooked fish flopped, jumped, and fought, but not for very long once we had them on. Kevin gave encouragement any time there was a fish on, demonstrated patience if a fish got off, and offered congratulations when a fish was reeled to the boat. Each time he reached into its mouth with a pair of pliers and extricated the hook from the fish's lips and then set it free.

We were in fifteen feet of water at the mouth of Skilak Lake and to perk us up Kevin issued an alert. "Be ready," he said. "There are some monsters here." He was not talking about great white sharks, but monster-sized trout. Moments later my rod dipped and the fight was on. Big fish. I could tell that, but Kevin wasn't sure what kind of fish it was. The behavior didn't line up with rainbow trout reactions. The fish pulled and fought, straining the twelve-pound test line.

I didn't know how big it was and I certainly didn't know what it was once Thurman raised the topic of the catch being something other than a rainbow. He was right. When the fish showed itself, we could identify it—a Dolly Varden. It was a twenty-three-inch Dolly. Technically called a "Dolly Varden trout," although I've never heard anyone verbally append *trout* to the name, Dolly Varden are pretty neat fish, another jewel of the Kenai River.

The fish were active. Soon after I had another hit from what again seemed to be a pretty large fish. It was full of life and leaping and we could see it was a rainbow as it shot out of the water, and a rainbow of considerable girth, a fat boy. It was a smart fish, too, making a run under the boat as I tried to turn him. But the move was its undoing. He came at the boat and that enabled Thurman to nab him in the net. The rainbow trout was as big as the Dolly— twenty-three inches. What a beautiful fish. We sent him on his way, back to the Kenai's depths.

I was convinced my next hit was an even bigger fish, but Thurman, being a little sharper, noted that I had actually hooked a rock. Rather strangely I did both. I was hung up on a rock, but I also had a fish on. Somehow it worked out. The hook was freed from the rock and the fish came in, probably a twenty-inch rainbow.

It was steady action for Lyman and me. Every bite we had was a rainbow for a while. Some were less than twenty inches long, some more. You couldn't always tell from the fight. Some bigger ones were fairly passive. Some smaller ones were tenacious.

"Sometimes those little scrappers fight harder than the big boys," Thurman said.

Boom, boom, Meacham was catching them fast. "Lyman's on fire!" Thurman declared.

The tease of our presentation was working. The fish liked what they saw and they attacked in hopes of gaining an easy snack or meal.

"Oh, they're hungry," Thurman said. "They're on the bottom and they're lazy fish. If it's two feet away from them they won't eat it, but if it's nearby they will go after it."

If we fished for a while and the fish didn't bite Thurman was quick to change the setup. Those hundreds of flies tied over the winter? It seemed he brought all of them with him. Thurman's tackle box was the size of a suitcase and he would probably never run out of choices. "Everything but the kitchen sink," is the way he described what he hauled to the river in the box.

There had been a lull between Lyman's catches and he said he felt well-rested. So much so that when the next fish fought on, Thurman urged him to put more oomph into his effort. "Are you saying I have to stand up?" Lyman asked. He did and the fish came in.

We slowly approached a gravel bar. There was a busy eagle parked there chowing down, dissecting a rainbow with its beak and claws. The eagle picked away and as we slid closer the bird chomped on raw fish. Seagulls flew in from the other side and spooked the eagle and we were coming up behind him. Too much of a crowd, he decided. The eagle clamped down on the dead trout and carried the carcass off. You could tell it took some work because the dead fish weighed down the hungry bird as he flapped his wings. The eagle only flew about fifty yards, but it was on the opposite shore on the edge of the woods. Surely he felt better protected.

"That was probably bigger than any rainbow we caught today," Lyman said as he watched the eagle tote the prey away.

We caught fish. They didn't bite in clusters, but every few minutes some interest was demonstrated. Kevin could humble you, though. The preceding September Kevin and a friend caught twenty-eight rainbow trout of twenty-four inches or longer. That ranked very high on the excitement meter to the point they became blasé about those shorter two-foot-long ones.

Another time fishing here with a friend, Thurman said the other guy fell asleep in his seat. "As soon as he does a big fish hits," Thurman said. "I laugh my head off. The rod drops overboard and he wakes up, jumps up, and reaches over and gets the rod. He's the luckiest son of a gun."

The cataraft was gliding toward a gravel bar with a known history of being a haven for rainbows. "Be on your toes, gents," Thurman said.

I made a long, arching cast of the type I only periodically complete neatly without the line tangling. It was a high, fly ball cast. It's going, it's going, it's gone. It was picturesque and darned if a fish didn't bite the moment the hook hit the water. "I think you've got a seagull," Lyman joked about the high flight of the cast. Nope, I had another rainbow trout on.

Lyman threw out his own high cast that Thurman made fun of, but which also hooked a fish. The struggle began. Lyman reeled, the fish fought back. "It hasn't come up yet," Meacham said, "but it's a Dolly Varden."

"That ain't no Dolly," Thurman said. He was correct again. Lyman had himself a twenty-two-inch rainbow trout. "That's a beauty," I said. "Ooh, nice," Thurman said.

Lyman hit a hot streak and I caught another little rainbow. Thurman guided the cataraft up and down the river. If fish didn't bite in what he considered to be a reasonable period of time, sometimes as short as ten minutes, he moved us elsewhere.

"The key to catching a lot of fish is covering a lot of water," said Thurman, who estimated we covered forty miles on the river that day. "Moving a lot, that's the key to my technique."

Lyman and I caught twenty-three fish between us, almost identically split. The biggest fish was twenty-three inches long. Kevin didn't want us to tell anyone how many fish we caught or where. Tell 'em you caught a few fish, if anybody asks, he said.

"I don't give away many secrets," Thurman said.

WHERE HAVE ALL THE KINGS GONE?

"As of June 12, all indices used to assess the abundance of early-run king salmon in the Kenai River indicate a run that is well below average. All Department assessment methods are running below the minimum in season management objectives at this time. The Department believes early-run king salmon that have yet to return to the Kenai River this season are needed to achieve adequate escapement for future production."

With that statement the Alaska Department of Fish and Game declared a ban on normal king salmon fishing on the Kenai River from 12:01 A.M., June 15 to 11:59 P.M., June 30. Only catch and release was permitted under the order in certain areas and not even catch and release in some others. For the king salmon late run, beginning at 12:01 A.M. on July 1 and continuing to 11:59 P.M. July 14 the catch and release order was to remain in effect with no bait or scent allowed.

We had been complaining about and wondering about the lack of king salmon in the river in May. Well, Fish and Game made it official that there really was a lack of king salmon in the river, not a perception.

This decree was based on the sonar counts taken at mile 8.6 on the river that measured how many fish entered the Kenai from Cook Inlet. According to historical totals, between 2002 and 2011 the average return of early-run king salmon to the Kenai was just shy of 12,000 fish. As of June 15, with the operating assumption that half of the run was over, only 1,333 fish had been counted. By June 22, the total was at just 4,000. Analysis indicated "the projections for all indices would be the lowest on record." The escapement goal is 5,300 to 9,000 fish.

Taking this step basically shut down king salmon fishing on the Kenai. Few anglers would trek to the river to fish when all odds were against them catching a fish and in addition being required to release it. As it was, it was hard enough for anyone to catch a king. State studies show that normally one king is caught for every forty-two hours of fishing with a guide, or for every fifty-two hours by an unguided individual. Making it harder, discouraging even making attempts, was the idea, of course. Fish and Game's directive was based on the goal of helping the species long-term. The numbers supported the drastic action.

Fish and Game's declaration produced much chatter on the Internet. "Fish and Game can't just twiddle their fingers and hope that minimum escapement will happen," read one posting. "Action HAS to be taken before the problem gets this severe. Sure, many sportfishers, as well as fishing guides, will throw a fit, but the question that has to be asked is, Do you value your resource enough to make the hard choices that need to be made?"

Another post read, "Let every angler who loves to fish think what it would mean to him to find the fish were gone?"

Well, the fish were gone, at least for the time being. The consequences were these: Millions of dollars were lost in business for fishing guides who counted on robust king salmon seasons for their living; millions of dollars were lost in Soldotna and the immediate area in hotel and restaurant revenue. Also, the idea of the Kenai River without king salmon represented a blow to local pride, as if something had been stolen from the Kenai Peninsula.

People wanted reasons. People wanted answers. But there were no definitive explanations available. A few years earlier it was revealed that much of Fish and Game's data revolving around counting kings was suspect because of the placement of the sonar counter. Scientists believed that the counter was too close to the mouth of Cook Inlet and threw into doubt the accuracy of the number of kings entering the river. The belief was that kings not only sometimes massed near the counter, but traveled back and forth across the line where they registered. That meant many kings were counted twice and that there were not nearly as many kings coming into the river each year in recent years as people thought. It was possible that the Kenai was being overfished for several years without the knowledge of Fish and Game, the public, anglers, or guides.

The point was that nobody knew. There was much more that nobody knew. The king salmon population returning to the Kenai River might have been diminished by foreign ocean trawlers. They scooped up huge amounts of fish for market while targeting other species and harmed the king population with an accidental (and to them irrelevant) bycatch. Or a change in the ocean temperature might be impacting kings. Or a rise in ocean acidity, which had been documented, impacted kings. Or perhaps the problem was all of the above. It was a frustrating situation and while there may have been a will to fix it, there was nothing tangible that someone could reach out and fix— whatever it was.

The lives of king salmon are pretty much a mystery to humans. The fish may be hatched in the Kenai River one year and typically not return for three to four years for most of them, and up to seven years for the really big ones. But nobody really knows what happens in those undocumented years. They could swim far, far away, or swim in circles. They could take up guitar playing or basketball. There was a widespread belief that there was no problem in the Kenai River that would have a major impact on the species when they are born. If there had been a concern, some years ago it was pretty much alleviated by the attention and work put into habitat conservation and preservation. Problems in the ocean, in saltwater, seemed more likely and that could be lack of sustenance in areas where currents changed.

Gut reaction seemed to place blame on foreign trawlers that have become more sophisticated and efficient in gathering the species of fish they are after, such as pollock, and merely discarding king salmon that are accidentally caught. As many as 122,000 king salmon were counted as bycatch in 2007, up from an average of nearly 38,000 between 1990 and 2001. New regulations limiting the king salmon bycatch went into effect in 2012 and demonstrated a dramatic cut in the waste. But no one knows if that was too late to help, either.

Although nobody is sure of this answer either, it is not impossible that the drop in the numbers of kings coming into the Kenai River is merely cyclical and this is a low point with the numbers naturally going to increase over the next five years or so. It is possible, too, that the implementation of rules governing the pollock bycatch will show positive effects over the next few years.

There is no doubt that there are a heap of maybes involved in this entire management process, but it was clear that sportfishermen and commercial fishermen (who lost openings) were hamstrung by the numbers and Fish and Game 2012 actions.

Someone caught in the crossfire, someone at ground zero and riding point for the department, was Robert Begich, the same biologist who delivered the lecture on how to fish the Kenai River at the Sportsman Show in April.

"Never a dull moment," Begich said later in the summer. "You think you have all of the time in the world [to cope with a shrinking number of kings] and then you don't. Things happen fast. There's no answer."

Instate data that tracked the runs and the spawners from 2006, 2007, and 2008, the years these kings would have been born that were expected to return to the Kenai in 2012 "were decent years. It wasn't the spawning escapement." By that Begich meant enough salmon were born during that period in the river to sustain a solid return. So that indicated something happened to the population after leaving the river and entering the saltwater.

"There has been persistent cooling of the Bering Sea and the Gulf of Alaska," Begich said. "We don't exactly understand what effect that has on the king stocks. Then there's the pollock bycatch. It's all West Coast and Canada stocks affected by that. It's not just Cook Inlet. They did change the quotas.

"You can't point to one thing and say when we do this we'll have good king runs again. It's very apparent that it's a big change, but we don't know exactly what it is."

No telling if global warming is involved or weird climate change.

"We're seeing birds later into the fall and the orange frost in Florida," Begich said. "Environmental things. You can't do anything about it. You can't control them. All we can do is manage conservatively."

For the devoted Kenai River angler the disappearance of the king salmon and all of the government regulation is like white noise on a radio, interfering with a pleasurable activity and turning it into an annoying situation. No one could fault Fish and Game for taking drastic steps, not even the Kenai River SportFishing Association. The position of that group, echoed by its founder Bob Penney, was simple. The same type of closures applied to sportfishermen had to be applied to commercial fishermen. If there weren't enough fish for sportsmen then there weren't enough fish period. The situation was closely monitored and commercial fishermen did lose days. Everyone did take a hit.

"Fish come first," Penney said once more.

CATCH AND RELEASE

On a Sunday in mid-June Bob Penney, Billy Saddler, a young man who works for him, and I, climbed into Bob's boat docked just outside his home at mile 23.2 on the Kenai River for a few hours of catch and release king salmon fishing. We were accompanied by Penney's six-year-old, well-behaved chocolate Labrador retriever named Killey, as in the Killey River, a Kenai tributary.

Sundays are guideless, anyway, and with the new rules in effect we didn't expect to see many other fishermen. Shortly after 6 A.M. a man Penney recognized as a retired guide was fishing just beyond the windows. We were a little later starting. It was sunny, but only thirty-nine degrees in a summer that really wasn't much of one.

There had been a slot limit allowing fishermen an exception to catch and keep a trophy fish, but that wasn't permitted just now. "This will be the first time in thirty-four years I haven't caught a king salmon," said Penney, meaning a keeper during the entire season.

We had three rods out and Penney remained convinced one of us would hook a king despite their scarcity. He was informing us how he, the captain, would handle it. When the rod bent, he would accelerate using his fifty-horse Yamaha to set the hook.

Penney did not disagree with Fish and Game's actions. They had to do it, he said, given the escapement numbers. The statistics are "the Holy Grail. They are sacred." He called the department ruling a "huge response" to the situation. "Escapement comes first so we'll continue to have this species."

The revelations about the older numbers cataloged by the sonar counter were troubling because they had long served as the basis for management decisions.

"They've been used on the Kenai for twenty-five years," Penney said. "Many anglers have questioned those sonar numbers in the past. It turns out now the department has realized they have been inaccurate."

Changes in the way the counts were made were implemented over the preceding couple of years, but it's hard to make apples and apples comparisons with the old numbers that can be believed. To Penney, this means that Fish and Game is managing the resource with "SWAG, a Scientific Wild-Assed Guess. The kings have come into the river, sniffed around, and went back out. They've overcounted the fish because they came in and out. Across Alaska the king runs are less than they used to be and nobody knows why."

I was no smarter than anyone else in attempting to pinpoint the right reason for the Kenai River king shortage this spring and summer of 2012, but I could tell Penney right then that the shortage was affecting us. None of us, not Bob, not Billy, not me, had a nibble on this fine day on the water. To release a king, first you have to catch one and that wasn't happening.

Penney was all for installing farther upriver a new sonar counter at a cost of around $2 million that scientists think would provide more accurate counts. "It's never too late," he said. "It's never too late to try."

Penney was not opposed to catch and release fishing at the moment. He has done it before and said he knows that at least three times he has caught the same king twice in different years in the same spot on the river. I'm not sure what fish markings told him that although I am pretty sure the fish didn't say, "You again?"

"I've done plenty of catch and release," Penney said. "Let's pick one up right now."

"Does that mean you want me to jump in and wrestle one?" I asked.

"I want you to catch a fish," Penney said.

Les Anderson's record was in no danger from me, catch and release or not. Billy told a story about an alleged 130-pound king caught by a commercial fisherman in a net the previous July in the Kasilof River nearby. A friend said, "You gotta see this." Billy said, "Jesus Christ, you got a shark in there?" His reaction: "Holy Toledo! Holy fox trot!"

Naturally, Billy informed Bob about this event.

"I've been waiting for a picture of it for a year," Penney said. "I was hoping it had fins. The guy was five-foot-eight holding it up and the tail was still bent on the ground. I'd pay $25,000 to catch that fish."

The woods were beautiful in the sunlight as the day warmed. They were at the height of their greenery after a cold spring, spruce, alder, birch, some hemlock, yellow cedar.

"I never get tired of hooking kings," Bob said. "I go other places fishing for kings (turns out he has accepted some elsewhere invitations) and they're fun and I respect it, but there's nothing like hooking a sixty- or seventy-pound king. Any other place to go fishing is second or third place to the Kenai."

Penney urged us to hook a fifty-five-pound king right then and let the current carry us around the bend as we fought it. "I'm doing the best I can," Saddler said. I could say the same. "Do they listen to you?" I asked Penney, wondering if he had a special psychic connection to the fish. He shook his head no. "It's my theory they don't speak English," he said.

For a moment Penney enjoyed what almost seemed to be a reverie about the good old days. About twenty years earlier, he said, in a boatload of anglers fishing near the popular Big Eddy spot in the river, they had eighty-eight king strikes and hooked thirty-seven kings in a single day. He is aware that sounds more like fantasy than reality. "The next day we went out and fished for five hours and never had a strike," he said.

By 9 A.M. we had been out for a few hours and passed the local eagle. Bob's neighborhood eagle hangs out on a tree near his home. Normally, when Penney has a successful fishing trip he fillets the salmon at water's edge and throws the head and guts in. The eagle knows to watch for such freebies.

"Right now he's saying, 'Where my breakfast?'" Penney said. "I've had him dive down so close I could feel the air in my hair from his wings."

Apparently seeing better pickings, the eagle took off upriver and flying with purpose banked to the left, skirted shore, and dove into the river to grab a fish in his mouth and talons. He settled at the edge of the riverbank just across from us and chomped down on the dead fish. The bird washed down his food with a drink of water, flew along the shore, and picked the top of another tree for a rest. With no other people around, the eagle was our only competition for catching fish. The eagle seemed to be on the lookout for more fish, dead or alive, perhaps still hungry for dessert.

Saddler got a king on, but lost it, our only sign of fish. Saddler, thirty, lives in Soldotna, where his family owns a bed and breakfast. He has been in Alaska for twelve years and loves it. He had the bright idea of asking Killey, who is a very smart dog, to find us a fish. "Go fetch!" he said. Good thought, but that didn't work.

There's no doubt that Saddler has great respect for Killey's intelligence. As we talked he sometimes spelled out words because he was sure the dog could understand him saying things he didn't want the dog to know. We were really hoping Killey could spell F-I-S-H. But it turned out he couldn't spell it any better than we could. We returned to land without king salmon.

THE RUSSIAN RIVER RED FRENZY

The Kenai River is famous for super-sized king salmon, but for a select few weeks over the summer it is also world famous for a bizarre scene on the Russian River tributary that is summed up with the illustrative phrase "combat fishing."

While Alaska cartoonist Chad Carpenter has drawn a panel that has a fisherman arriving at the river in a tank, that is satire. The real thing is offbeat enough. To fish the Russian River when the sockeye, or red salmon, enter the

Kenai from the ocean is to set aside all ingrained images of peace, tranquillity, and solitude while fishing. Anglers crowd finite space elbow to elbow. Those who cast must be cautious not to hook either themselves in the back of the head or the person standing next to them.

Unlike king salmon, red salmon return to the river by the hundreds of thousands at a minimum and quite often as many as 1.2 million of the fine-eating, thrashing fish in two distinct runs in June and July. The red run is not about catching trophy fish. It is about catching eating fish, about bringing home dinner. The red fishery is basically an Alaska fishery. Tourists may fish for sockeye if they are around, but rarely do they fly in just for reds. And the fish really are red in freshwater, although they are silver when in the ocean. Chinook and coho salmon are silver-sided. Reds in the Kenai are mostly red. They have wider mouths than those other species, and pointier faces, too. Sockeyes are much smaller than kings and generally smaller than silvers. A ten-pound sockeye is a treat.

For one thing it is difficult to time the fishery. One minute the river is void of fish, the next minute they are pouring in so thick that you can stand on shore or cruise past in a raft or boat and see nothing but red beneath the shallowest of waters. It is jaw-dropping to watch the parade of fish swim past, a rare experience in nature if you are actually standing in water wearing waders and have the fish swarm past your feet. Because of the bounty of so many fish arriving, the rules for catching them are different as well. Usually, anglers can keep three reds per day.

Fishing for reds is a bonanza of action. They are aggressive and bite much more often than kings. They provide a good fight, but not one that is going to make you feel as if you have just been weight lifting with Arnold Schwarzenegger. It's all about timing. When the fish come, you had better be flexible enough to show up. The Russian River is the most popular fishing spot, where the best fishing is, and it is located about 120 miles from Anchorage.

People who have real-life jobs have been known to declare holidays, call in sick, or simply head out of the city after work, drive to the river and then stay up all night fishing before going right back to work the next day. The lure of the sockeye is powerful and the combat fishing scene must be witnessed once in a lifetime.

The Russian River is thirteen miles long in the Kenai Mountains and it drains into the Kenai River at Cooper Landing. Access is the biggest challenge to the Russian. When word spreads that the reds are in, the winding, two-lane Sterling Highway can be transformed into a creep-along traffic jam. Fishermen park willy-nilly along the side of the highway and create their own paths walking along the road to the fishing grounds. Safety is forgotten, so the wise driver is advised to slow to five miles per hour in stretches.

Those who park along the road either do not wish to pay the parking fee of $11.25 or they have been shut out of the jammed lots. Hundreds of cars cram into official parking areas. Once situated, fishermen have another challenge. The trick of fishing the Russian River is that the fish pass by hugging the opposite bank. There is no automotive or foot access to the area where the fish are. To reach the far bank anglers ante up $10.25 for space on a ferry that carries them across the water a distance of only 100 yards or so.

It is there where the fishermen claim their posts, perhaps about twelve feet apart. They carve out a little piece of territory and cast. Some even just sit down on the dirt of the bank and wait for others to catch their limit and vacate their spot. On this sunny June day, one of the most spectacular, pure days of summer at seventy degrees, that could take a while, though, because the height of the run had not been reached and limits had to be worked for, not assumed.

The green ferry itself is no everyday boat. It is essentially an open-air barge, perhaps fifty feet long, crossing the turquoise waters back and forth, 100 yards at a time, critically attached to a cable so that it doesn't glide away with the current. Ferry trips are a two-man operation, one man on each side. About thirty-five orange life jackets hang on empty frame sides, just in case something goes wrong with a ferry full of people.

The current ferry system is a successor to an idea introduced by an original entrepreneur in the 1930s. A big-game guide named Hank Lucas used a rowboat to transfer fishermen to the south side of the river. This cable ferry system replaced that method and the ferry carries about twenty people at once each way at peak times. By my watch, a one-way trip took about one minute and ten seconds.

Given the shortness of the ride, and the very limited amount of time that it operates—pretty much a couple of weeks in June and a couple of weeks in July—the Russian River ferry is somewhat of an oddity. But it is an iconic oddity,

The Russian River ferry is the way those in pursuit of sockeye salmon get across the narrow body of water when those fish return to spawn in June and July.

a well-known one, and it apparently has a constituency that loves it more than resents it judging by the souvenirs for sale by the ticket booth. For purchase there are Russian River ferry sweatshirts for $32, caps for $20, and T-shirts for $18. Also available are Russian River ferry "Shut Up And Fish" T-shirts.

Russian River activity was not especially heated in mid-afternoon. Some fishermen had come and gone, because their limits were met, or they ran out of time. Families clustered at picnic benches enjoyed the scene. They were like spectators at a sporting event, on a pleasant outing with the kids. If they lived in any one of a number of other US locales they might have been at the beach this day. There are aluminum fish cleaning tables at water's edge for anglers who got lucky, and after they climb off the ferry and before they climb back into their cars, they clean their catch.

Tim Miller of Anchorage, an Oregon transplant, was used to fishing alone before he moved to Alaska and he said it is not as much fun fishing with crowds. "The only thing that makes this worthwhile is the size of the fish," Miller said.

He had fished the night before and fished this afternoon and he had four reds for the road, with a twenty-six incher his biggest. "I'm happy," Miller said.

Clearly, the peak of the run had not hit yet, though Miller noticed more fishermen had caught their limit of three the day before than on this day. "It's OK, just OK," Miller said of the pace. "It's not bad."

Teddy Haunen of Seward was done for the day, too, with two sockeye in the bag after fishing from 7 A.M. until about 3 P.M.

"It was spotty," he said. "Every fifty casts I caught one. One every two-and-a-half hours." Actually his timing was off. The gap between bites was a bit larger. "It's a little too early. When they're packed in it's a pretty fun time."

For the most part Haunen loves the Kenai River. He is attracted by "The peace. You're here with nature and God and the sound of the water. And cold feet. It's worth it. It helps you escape everything."

Then there is combat fishing during these short weeks on the Russian. "This is an experience you've got to do," he said. "Not everybody follows the proper etiquette, though. I was on the bank and I was being a gentleman waiting my turn and then I caught a fish and reeled it in. And someone slipped right into our hot spot."

Not nice. Someone with a short temper might be provoked into a nasty confrontation. "There are some people like that," Haunen said. "I just dealt with it. I'm here to catch fish."

The Russian River fishing experience is a tradition for many, just a wild aspect of fishing on the Kenai Peninsula that they got used to with all of its crowds and quirks that they wouldn't put up with elsewhere.

A group of more or less middle-aged friends from Anchorage and Eagle River make annual pilgrimages to the Russian River as a team and they were taking a break in the parking lot by their vehicles, which included a sleeping camper. They had food, they had drink, they had all the necessary gear. They were equipped for a few days of hard-core red salmon fishing. How often do they make this getaway?

"Not often enough," said John Landt.

That would probably be the lament of most fishermen who actually have to work to make a living. This was a gang of fly fishermen, members of the Alaska Fly Fishers, with their own flies, using that long-cast method much of the average world has only seen in *A River Runs Through It*. They make their own runs to the Kenai a couple of times a year. The preceding fall they all caught rainbow trout.

"I was fishing for kings and I caught a red," noted Mike Harsh.

The quartet of friends knew they were pushing their luck by hitting the Russian on this gorgeous weather weekend—just a little too soon for the big run—but they wanted to come, so they came. "Today was just a day we wanted to have fun," said Keven Kleweno, "to be together and enjoy fishing."

Not everybody has to catch as many fish as possible. They were there for the overall experience. My kind of guys. Fly fishing is not my thing. I am not good at it and I feel that any time I cast I am likely to hook a

tree branch, wrap the line around some solid object, or pierce someone's forehead with a hook.

"We can teach you to cast in an hour," Kleweno said. I could envision what an ugly, frustrating hour that would be. I would stick to bait casting. These anglers were also part of Project Healing, a much more worthwhile endeavor than trying to take the kinks out of my casting motion. Project Healing is a nonprofit organization that works with wounded warriors, soldiers back from the wars in Afghanistan and Iraq who could use some R&R. The group organizes fly fishing outings for servicemen and their families. It was in the third summer of operation.

This is what combat fishing on the Russian River looks like, with anglers elbow to elbow, at water's edge when the sockeye salmon return in force in midsummer.

"We have a lot of guides who step up and donate trips," Harsh said of the Kenai River participants. "Our warriors don't pay for anything. It's probably one of the most rewarding things I've ever done."

The four men came to the Russian for reds over the weekend so they could share a good time. But they were savvy enough to recognize the downside of combat fishing, too. Too many people tightly packed in too small an area going after the same fish, and worse, not all of them being polite about it. That was the biggest gripe. Like Haunan, Frank Stevens, Harsh, and Kleweno saw more rude behavior every year.

"Combat fishing isn't really fun," Stevens said.

"Combat fishing is dangerous," Harsh said. "I have dodged a hook going by my nose. Some people don't know river etiquette."

There's that word again. When someone has a fish on, those nearby are supposed to reel in so lines do not tangle. Some fishermen don't cooperate, they said. When they catch fish and move along the shore to help them reel in, others steal their spots and refuse to give them back.

"You see that more and more," Kleweno said.

Harsh sighed. "That's combat fishing," he said.

Yet the lure of tasty sockeye salmon is a strong one and they all admit they would like to bring reds home.

"In my family, the first choice for eating is reds," Kleweno said. "I'll take a day off in the middle of the week when it's less crowded, put in six or seven hours and I'll come off the river with three nice fish."

That explained the attraction and why fishermen are willing to put up with the combat part: three reds in a day make for several excellent meals. "That's a lot of it," Stevens said.

I knew exactly what they were talking about. My favorite salmon recipe of all, cooking king salmon with a teriyaki sauce, came from Bob Penney. My favorite salmon dish to order in any restaurant anywhere was salmon fettuccini, made with grilled red salmon pieces.

At the intersection of the Sterling Highway and the Kenai Spur Road, there used to be a restaurant that opened as the Four Seasons. It was a little place in the trees with cloth tablecloths and low lighting. Believe it or not, THE Four Seasons restaurant in New York got wind of it and threatened to sue over use of the name. The proprietor, Geri Litzenberger, who was also the cook much of the time, decided she could do without a legal battle and changed the name to Through The Seasons. But she didn't change the menu. I was addicted to that dish. Every time I fished on the Kenai I had to stop for dinner to eat that fettuccini/red salmon dish. I kept telling myself that I needed to try something else, but when it came time to order, I never could.

Eventually, the restaurant went out of business and the dish disappeared from my life. I've never seen it anywhere else and I still think of it as probably the best dish I've ever eaten in a restaurant.

That night I ate dinner at another Kenai institution, Sal's Diner. Just to prove its true-blue Kenai River connection, the newspaper-like menu has a picture of Les Anderson on the back accompanied by the story of how he caught his record fish. Les, you can't duck the fish.

Known for its large portions and being open twenty-four hours a day, the Soldotna restaurant is not nearly as upper-class as Through The Seasons was, but it serves hearty food. Occasionally, it indulges its clients with a challenge. Not quite the same as an event on the competitive eating circuit, like the Coney Island hot-dog eating showcase on July 4, but a fresh contest was certainly of appeal to the amateur stuff-your-face crowd.

This was the deal: Eat a Sal's five-pound cinnamon roll, topped off by a glass of milk, within forty-five minutes and it was free of charge and you got your picture on the Wall of Fame. Otherwise it cost $21.99. The contest was new, so there was only one winner to date. I got up from my table and wandered over to the glass case housing desserts. Not having met a five-pound cinnamon roll before, I was duly impressed to see that it was pretty much equal to eating an entire cake.

Following the general rule that it is not wise to eat anything bigger than your head, I was not tempted. I did order the normal cinnamon roll, though, which measured a few inches by a few inches and was a filling enough portion. Quite tasty, too. But I still would rather have been eating that fettuccini with red salmon.

Only one day after I visited the Russian River and talked to anglers who said the sockeye had not completely hit, Fish and Game reported a twenty-four-hour count of 230,000 reds pouring into the Kenai River. The first run was in full flower.

FISHING SCHOOL

Dave Atcheson sat in a booth in bustling Sullivan Arena at the Sportsman Show, passing out brochures to passersby, talking up the glories of the Kenai River. The coordinator of the Kenai River Fishing Academy, he was rounding up students for the June bait-casting class and the July fly fishing class.

The weeklong June course, instruction, room and board, lectures, and Kenai fishing all included, cost $2,185 per person for a concentrated education on bait casting the Kenai and in July cost $150 more per week for know-how on fly fishing on the Kenai.

Wisely, the Academy's advertising indicates that the course does not promise someone who enrolls that they will catch a king salmon. It does promise to improve skills: "Give us one week and you'll be on your way to successful Alaskan trips in the future—an Educated Angler."

An offspring of Kenai Peninsula College, the summer sessions originated in 2003 and have proven popular particularly given that the cost is a bit higher than your average weekend in Soldotna. The idea sprung from the mind of Gary Turner, who is now director of the college, but Atcheson currently handles the nuts and bolts.

"The goal is to educate anglers on not just how to fish, but on the river history," Atcheson said. "There's definitely a conservation ethic involved and a big biology component."

Turner is retired military from Bellevue, Washington, who made many trips to Alaska and spent five years trying to catch a king salmon with no luck before he dreamed up the educational program. "I compared it to golf clinics in Arizona," Turner said. "They go out and practice what they've learned. I started writing a curriculum."

Outfitters he mentioned the idea to were all for it. Turner incorporated many safety elements, from behavior in boats and cold water survival to dealing with bears.

"Little things like that that can save their lives," he said.

The Academy program has been a hit from the start, though there has been fine-tuning. It began with classes of sixteen, but was reduced to twelve, Turner said, to ensure that people got enough individual attention. It was a balancing act for him, as well. As a nonprofit, the goal was not to make money, but he also couldn't lose money on the program either. Repeat customers return all of the time. One young man got the course for a high school graduation present.

"He said, 'I want to be a guide when I grow up,'" Turner said. "We gave him a start."

The courses have space for twelve people at a time and if more than $2,000 sounds like a lot of money, Atcheson said that's what it costs to put on the seminar programs. A full-day float of the Kenai River is part of the package and so is a fly-in fishing trip elsewhere on the Kenai Peninsula.

There is a lot of word of mouth in the program, Atcheson said, and perhaps surprisingly, there are repeat customers who view the entire experience not merely as an educational opportunity, but as a vacation. Indeed, newcomers to fishing are attracted to the courses, but so are old-time Alaskans and visitors from overseas who have heard about the wonders of the Kenai River who rather than just blindly picking a guide service, opt for this more structured setting.

Certainly, there are other bodies of water in the area, and the course tiptoes into them at times, but the appeal, it should be no surprise, is the Kenai River above all. The name carries magic. The name carries clout. The name is the lure.

"It's kind of a storied river," Atcheson said. "It's so accessible. People have heard about it."

Atcheson is more organizer than full-time teacher in the program. He is forty-eight, originally from Cortland, New York, and moved to Alaska in 1984. He is a very avid fisherman and spends as much time as possible on the Kenai in the summer months.

When he was younger and working in Seward he joined fellow cannery workers for a sockeye fishing trip an hour or so away on the Russian River and was spellbound. "Fishing for reds, I had never seen anything like it," Atcheson said. "The combat fishing was something to behold."

In the mid-1990s, Atcheson worked for Fish and Game, and part of his job was to fly fish for rainbow trout. "I thought, 'I can do that,'" he said. "I got paid to fish ten hours a day. It was a total dream job." Being out on the Kenai River day after day gave him a supreme appreciation for the body of water.

The 2012 bait-casting class ran from June 17 to June 22. Before that Atcheson got some of his own fishing in and despite the shortage of king salmon he had already caught two kings, one about ten minutes after he began fishing. One fish was a thirty pounder. The other was just shy of fifty inches and about fifty pounds. "There were a lot of fish around that day," he said.

It might have been the only day of the spring that was true. Soon enough Fish and Game had put the clamps on the fishery. Atcheson lucked out with his early season success.

Atcheson was reporting in to me at the college building where the campers were due to begin the course that evening and I was hanging out for the first day of school to talk to people who were mostly strangers to the Kenai. Informational packets with the schedule were passed out. Get-to-know-you personal backgrounds were exchanged.

Not everyone was a complete stranger to the river, however. Fred and Ruth Ganske, a couple that might have been in their sixties from Llano County, Texas, the Texas hill country where they fish all of the time, were attending for the third straight year. This was a duo who viewed the Academy as their hosts for what was essentially a guided vacation. "It's a hoot," said Ruth.

The Ganskes checked out the course online, read up a little on the Kenai River via the Internet, and thought they'd give the school a try. "It surpassed all my expectations," she said. "We'll do it as long as we physically can."

Paul Sciera was from Colorado and signed up to follow in the footsteps of his brother, who had previously attended. It was Paul's first trip to Alaska and investigating the Kenai was definitely part of his fishing education. "I don't know much about fishing," he said. "I'm here to learn more."

Some of the gang had ventured to Homer and Kachemak Bay the day before for a long halibut fishing trip that cost them sleep. That was a good fishing warm-up and there was an air of excitement in the classroom.

Atcheson stepped up to the podium and asked a critical question. "Does everybody have a license?" Everybody better have a license when they set out on the Kenai River because one thing Fish and Game does not have a sense of humor about is anglers who haven't paid their dues.

Prices vary by age and residency status. An annual Alaska resident license in 2012 was a bargain at $24, plus $10 for a king salmon stamp. That is essentially a king salmon tax. Kids under sixteen fish for free—the idea is to encourage them to take up the sport. Nonresident anglers, like the Ganskes, Sciera, and me, faced higher costs. My fishing license for the year cost $145.

I could have purchased a salmon stamp for the season for $100, but opted for $10 per day. That was looking like the right choice because the restrictions on king fishing made it seem unlikely I would get to go out ten times.

One of the earliest students who signed up for the Academy class the first year was Dennis Gease, father of Ricky, the Sportfishing Association's executive director. Dennis was new to Alaska, so he was attracted to a crash course in adjusting to Kenai River fishing ways.

"I thought, 'Maybe I should do that,'" the elder Gease said. "It's a good vacation. Plus, you get the inside information. How to bait, how to fillet your fish, everything you need to know if you don't know the local customs."

That is a key point. Fishing is different in different parts of the United States. Anglers pursue different species in different regions. They use different bait, different lures, and different equipment. They fish at different times of the day, in different temperatures, for smaller fish than Chinook salmon and bigger fish, too, from muskie and marlin in the ocean.

The Academy specializes in teaching about all of those facets of fishing on the Kenai River. "I was basically a nonresident who was not familiar with Alaska fishing," Dennis said. "It was very worthwhile. A lot of fun. I caught the first king in the class. I think it was forty-two pounds. I also caught a nice lingcod. That was a bonus prize."

Of course landing a very impressive-sized king as a beginner tends to have a spoiling affect on an angler, or at least tends to leave the wrong impression about the challenge of finding them and hauling them in. "I thought this king fishing stuff is a snap," Dennis said. "I think I've caught three or four more in the years since."

At the lectern in the classroom for day one of this year's Academy sessions, Atcheson launched into an introductory lecture.

"There is good news and bad news," he said. "The good news is the weather report is really good. The bad news is the Kenai River has gone to catch and release. There are not a lot of fish [kings] coming in. That's a bummer."

One thing obvious in Atcheson's tone and words was his own passion for the Kenai. "I pretty much love to be outdoors," he said. "I feel the connection to something bigger than myself. I feel really awesome when I'm in the outdoors. Everything else disappears like the list of things you have to do. Nothings puts me more into that natural environment than when I'm fishing."

Most of the dozen participants were middle-aged. Some were from Asia. Some were Alaskans. There was a father-and-son team from Japan. When the twenty-something son introduced himself to say why he was there, he said, "I'm blessed to have a father who likes to fish and not knit." That kind of let us know who was paying the bill.

The group then met someone who was going to be very important in their lives over the coming days. Bo Ansel, operator of Bo's Fishing Guide Service & Lodging on the Kenai River since 1985, was in his tenth year as a primary instructor for the Academy. Ansel told the crowd a little bit about the fish on the Kenai that they might not know much about, from rainbow trout to Dolly Varden and a species they were bound to meet—pink, or humpy, salmon.

Pink salmon are on a different return cycle to the river than other salmon. Pinks come back once every two years instead of every year. They are not as coveted as Chinooks, silvers, or sockeyes. They are not regarded as that tasty. But they are abundant when they come in, often grabbing hooks meant for other salmon. Humpies are similar in size to reds, but may grow a larger fin on their backs that make them resemble hunchbacks. Their coloration is a mix of silver and red. They are also characterized by large spots on the back and tail. During a pink year it is almost impossible to avoid catching some when going after silvers or reds. Guides tend to treat them as a nuisance, but for the uninitiated angler, the fight to bring in a humpy can be just as much fun as bringing in another type of salmon. There is a fifth type of salmon in Alaska, the chum, or dog salmon, but nobody eats them (they are sometimes fed to dogs) and while they are found on the Kenai Peninsula, they do not come into the Kenai River itself.

"If you catch them near the saltwater they can be fun to catch on light tackle," Ansel said of pinks.

The students trooped outside to the parking lot where Ansel located his truck with a trailer attached carrying one of his standard Kenai River boats. It was a show-and-tell production, with Ansel displaying eighty-pound test, a variety of lures, and even slicing sardines for bait.

Ansel was an enthusiastic instructor and said he has enjoyed his decade in the role. "I love it," he said. "What is exciting for me is I'm always learning and I tell them to do whatever works for me. You're always trying to fine-tune your capabilities."

Kenai River guide Bo Ansel has been working with the students at the Kenai Fishing Academy retreats for ten years and loves teaching people how to fish the famous river.

Ansel and Atcheson informed the crowd of a superstition that is taken seriously on Alaska waters. Actually, the banana superstition is far more widespread than just Alaska. I have run into it elsewhere and you can even Google "bananas fishing superstition" and it pops up immediately. No bananas on the boat in any shape or form will be tolerated. Guides have been known to throw bananas overboard if they discover them in anglers' backpacks. They even curse if they learn bananas were eaten at breakfast. This superstition dates back years.

Atcheson admitted that he was once guilty of a violation of this basic tenet of Alaska fishing. "I got in trouble for bringing banana bread," he said.

Ooh, bad boy.

The true origin of bananas bringing bad luck to fisherman may be lost to time. There is more than one theory, some far-fetched. Some say that bananas bringing bad luck to ships originated when African ships transported slaves in the holds of banana boats. That sounds a bit grim for something that is talked about so lightheartedly.

Then there is the story that bananas in the South Pacific were only fit for royalty and a commoner who partook of the fruit was penalized with death. Again, that seems to be a bit harsh to be applied to modern-day sportfishing.

I came across another website that featured a picture of a bunch of bananas inside one of those red circles with the slash across it in a discussion of boating superstitions.

This banana thing has never been a problem for me. I don't like bananas. I have eaten apples aboard Kenai River fishing boats with no criticism, so I'm thinking that's cool.

Ansel reported no student faux pas with bananas during the course. It all proceeded smoothly during the week and as far as he could tell a good time was had by all and much was learned.

"It went well," he said of the way this Academy group performed. "They seemed to learn a lot."

The students did just about everything but catch king salmon, which everyone hoped to do. "It was horrible," Ansel said of the king situation. "I think we're going to have this problem for a few years."

No one caught kings in this Academy class, but on the fly-in trip to Crescent Lake the group caught Dolly Varden and lake trout. Turner estimated that the fishing was so good that the students caught 300 dollies and 15 lake trout of at least fifteen pounds. "It was a fabulous trip," Turner said.

Each angler got to keep five fish and the action was so fast, he said, people commented that they were "tired of catching fish." Not something fishermen say very often. "It was so good it exhausts you."

ANOTHER SHOT AT KINGS

The hunt for king salmon resumed in a Harry Gaines fishing boat. This time my guide was twenty-year-old Cody Dutcher, one of Reuben Hanke's youngest guides. We were out on the Kenai River with Lacey Cashman, seventeen, from Soldotna, one of Cody's friends, and Ryan Lambourne, a precocious twelve-year-old from Cedar Hills, Utah, whose grandparents live on the river.

Ryan had never fished for king salmon before, but he had fished for reds, and in general he claimed to be a pretty avid fisherman. However, he said he had never been in a boat on a river like this before. Blond, with braces, and a wide, innocent smile, Ryan didn't look any older than his professed age even if his conversation made it seem he was going on thirty.

"The fish are coming this way, right?" he asked. We hope so. We definitely hope so.

"They're coming from the ocean," Cody noted.

Ryan seemed fairly knowledgeable about what was going on, the habits of king salmon, the catch and release rules, and he seemed far more mature than the average kid his age, but he also had a million questions and comments.

"I'd let it go anyway if I caught a big king, so it could spawn," he said.

"That's a good attitude to have, buddy," Cody said.

One of those general superstitions about fishing is that if you are in a boat with a kid, the kid catches fish before you do. Also, if you are in a boat with a woman, the woman catches fish before you do. I was doomed.

Cody guided us into a spot known as Fallin' In Hole. "Is that a good spot?" Ryan asked. Then, "I love fishing. It's my passion." I chuckled. It was early in the morning, but Ryan was well oiled with energy and enthusiasm.

Fully aware of what constituted a large Chinook salmon, Ryan announced

Cody Dutcher, at twenty, is one of Reuben Hanke's youngest guides at the Harry Gaines fish camp.

that if he caught a seventy-pound king it would pull him overboard because he only weighed seventy-two pounds.

"I'll catch you," Cody replied, immediately offering theoretical emergency backup.

Periodically, Ryan asked a jackpot question. "How come there aren't more fish?" he said. We had the choice of listing those many options Fish and Game was exploring, or we could just say, "Nobody knows."

There were not many fishermen out and about, but we knew the answer to the why of that.

"Does this mean the fishing is going to be bad for five years?" Ryan asked. Another million-dollar question with no accurate answer to offer.

Cody marveled at the empty water around us. There were no other fishing boats in sight on a pleasant summer day when there should have been fifty boats out pursuing king salmon at the height of the season.

"Are you sure it's not been overfished?" Ryan quizzed us. "I sure hope it's not being overfished. That would ruin everything."

Are you sure you're just twelve? That's what I wondered.

Then Ryan gave us his own theory about where the king salmon were that were scheduled to show up in the Kenai. "I think the salmon just got smarter and figured out they could build nests in the ocean and stay there," he said. "There could be 100-year-old salmon."

Perhaps Ryan should testify the next time some fisheries board holds hearings on the possible reasons why the king salmon stayed away. He would no doubt be as interesting to listen to as any scientist that didn't know the answer either.

Sometimes it is just fun to sit back and observe where a kid's mind roams. "Did you ever hit a fish with a boat?" Ryan asked Cody.

Turns out Cody did just that once on the Kasilof River. He was motoring along and heard a thump.

"You just stunned it, right?" I said.

"Nooo," Cody said. But the fish floated away before he could retrieve it.

Abruptly, we had big excitement on board. My rod dipped.

"Does he have a fish?" Ryan said.

Maybe at first, for a moment, I thought I did, but the pull felt wrong. A fish was not on my hook. Ryan's and my lines had drifted together and I caught his plug. False alarm.

Cody revved up the outboard and zipped us down the river to a fresh spot, one he hoped would be livelier. We huddled with our backs to the wind, hoods up to shield our heads, until we settled into the new hole. That brief break gave Ryan time to formulate more questions.

"Ever have a fish jump in the boat?" he asked Cody. "Ever have a fish jump next to the boat?"

There was another boat near us and an angler did have a fish on. From a distance we saw it leap out of the water.

"Oh, my gosh," Ryan said. He looked mighty impressed—for a moment. "Ever have everyone in the boat get one on at once?" That was an experience Cody had coped with. He was rowing a drift boat and two fishermen simultaneously hooked kings of roughly forty-five pounds. "That was crazy," Cody said.

Having Ryan in the boat was like being a baseball infielder with three people hitting grounders at you at once. You barely had time to grab one and throw to first before the next hit was winging at you. How long would it take to land a king if we caught one? How come Cody was guiding on the Kenai River now instead of the Kasilof? I liked Cody's answer. He said he had learned all he needed to know on the Kasilof and basically moved up to the big time, or the majors, as the case might be. "This is the big show with the big kings," he said.

Right about then, Ryan committed to a career choice.

"I'd like to have your job," he told Cody.

"I love it," Cody replied.

Not that Ryan dwelled on that. He was off in another direction, asking how it was that Cody knew about all of these special fishing holes we were trying out like Honeymoon Cove and Big Eddy. "I spend a lot of time on the water, buddy," he said.

Ryan's rod seemed to be bouncing up and down a little and he began reeling. Was there a fish there or not? Something seemed out of the ordinary. Ryan reeled in, but no fish was on the end of the line. "How did it get off?" he asked.

"It was not firmly hooked," I said.

"Guess not, boss," said Cody. Boss. He called me that several times and Ryan he called buddy. Lacey was pretty quiet the entire time and Cody didn't call her anything for short.

It is one thing to have almosts like that when kings are biting with some regularity. To have one within sniffing distance when there are almost none to be had and lose it is extra disappointing. Catching a Chinook salmon on the Kenai requires knowledge, experience, and a bit of luck and all three did not come together on Ryan's hit.

"It's hero or zero out there on the Kenai," Cody said. "On a tough day when you don't see many fish, one fish makes you a hero."

The water had been clearer a day earlier, but with all of the sunshine Cody felt the snowmelt had increased, rolling down from the mountains picking up debris and making the river a bit dirtier. That would make it harder for the fish to see the hooks.

At one point our rods vibrated so violently it seemed they had a nervous condition. But they were just bouncing off the rocky bottom. We paused at Sunken Island, one of those special river spots where fish often congregate. "There are always fish here," Cody said, "but you have to get them to bite." Oh yes, that old fundamental.

The kid's mind never stopped working. "Would you kill me if I dropped the pole into the water?" Ryan asked Cody. "What if I had a fish on so big that it pulled it out of my hand? Would you help me? I'm scared. I don't want to get pulled in."

"I'll help you," Cody pledged.

Actually, people do not fall out of boats into the Kenai River. It practically never happens. The water is not choppy. There are never big waves. The boats generally don't go that fast. Fishermen sit down when the boats are moving. To go swimming in the Kenai River you pretty much have to go in on purpose, like good old Dan Myers when he dove in chasing that ninety-pound king.

Ryan stood four-foot-something and calculated that if he caught a really large king salmon it would be bigger than him.

"If I catch a 112-pounder it will pull me in," he said.

"If you catch a 112-pounder I'll give you $100," Lacey said.

"If you catch a 100-pound fish, you'll be famous," Cody said.

If Ryan caught a world record he and Cody would be friends for life.

In his young life, Ryan had already dabbled in baseball, soccer, and lacrosse. He frequently rode a bicycle and regularly went fishing in Utah. "Fishing is my game," he said. But he confided in us, he actually had two

Ben Ellis is a past executive director of the Kenai River Sportfishing Association and is currently director of Alaska's state parks department.

passions, fishing, and eating carrots. "I once ate so many carrots that my teeth turned orange," Ryan said.

One way Ryan displayed his maturity was by not complaining about the lack of fish. Another youth would have declared boredom. Ryan understood what was happening.

"There are days that are a lot better than this," Cody said. "We're still fishing. We're still trying."

No kings were hooked. No fish were caught. Cody was pretty impressed with young Ryan's demeanor, though. "He's gonna go far," Cody said.

Thinking about how Ryan had embraced the notion of becoming a guide, I said, "At least you gave him purpose in life."

SALMON RUMINATING

It was a pretty, cool evening on the deck next to the cabins at the Harry Gaines fish camp with beers being sipped during what amounted to a round table. Owner Reuben Hanke and I sat gazing at the river along with Ben Ellis. Ellis, currently director of Alaska State Parks, used to have Ricky Gease's job as executive director of the Kenai River Sportfishing Association and that was after he was a newsman for the now-defunct *Anchorage Times*.

Ellis has been around the river for twenty years and like all of us was perplexed and concerned about the king salmon run of 2012. Ellis was actually just passing through, on his way to a business meeting in Homer the next day. Even if he wasn't fishing he reveled in quality time by the river.

"You can't get a better place than sitting by the river," Ellis said as he puffed on a cigar a few feet removed from one of the guest cabins he rented instead of an inland motel room. "I'm afraid we're seeing what a lot of us felt in the nineties. There were all of these kings we were seeing, seventy-pounders in fish boxes. We had questions about whether there was overfishing.

"Unfortunately, maybe the fishing was too liberal in the 1990s. I hope I'm wrong. Maybe this is a lull, a blip, or something, in the cycle. I don't know if we're any closer now than we were twenty years ago in knowing about these fish."

Ellis made a salient point. If everyone was guessing about the cause of a low early run, ticking off a list of choices from trawler interference to ocean diseases, then he was right. We don't know more than we did. Maybe we just have better theories.

"We don't know what might be stressing them in the ocean," Ellis said. "We should have a pretty good feeling what is happening in the river. We know there has been more habitat conservation and bank stabilization."

The admission two years ago that the sonar counter may not have been as accurate as everyone thought it was threw a lot of experts for a loop. Guides, the fishing experts on the scene day in and day out, had suspicions for a long time that something might not be right. There would be an announcement that the sonar count reported a large number of fish coming into the Kenai River, but at the same time the guides weren't seeing or catching fish that were supposed to be there. That combination added credence to the suggestion that fish were going back and forth beyond the counter line.

"You've got the milling factor," Ellis nodded. "They come in and they go back out." Admittedly, there have been doomsayers calling this the demarcation point, a dividing line announcing the end of an era on the Kenai River. But Ellis would not go along with that conviction. "I don't know that I'd be ready to call it that yet," he said. "What if next year we get a ton of fish coming in? We need the perspective of time. Is it the end of large fish in the Kenai River in large numbers? We don't know that yet."

Reuben said he had wondered about another aspect of the counts for a long time.

"What do you do when you get huge sockeye runs and kings are in [the river at the same time]?" he said. "We could have missed counts. We don't have a number. We had a day when 5,500 fish were supposed to be coming through the sonar and we did not have a net up [no fish were caught.]"

Even though it directly affects his livelihood, Reuben said, "I'm OK with a total closure in the Kenai because the fish come first." What he was not OK with was commercial fishermen still having their openings when "you can't even keep a fish."

Guides also had input into the management plan, so erroneous data affected their thinking, too. "We all built the management plan on the best available data," Reuben said. "We've managed the fish into the ground. We're all guilty, not just the department."

In the 1970s, there was no real Chinook salmon fishery. In the 1980s and 1990s, as Reuben said, it was, "Wow." On one trip in the nineties people in his boat hooked into sixteen king salmon. "I had the best day of my life in one shift. There was nothing like it."

Ellis was not inclined to believe that what seems to be a healthier river is to blame for the lack of kings. "I can't believe it's that part of it," he said. "You just wish you had X-ray vision."

I wondered aloud why some government agency didn't actually send frogmen out to gaze at life under the surface of the river, but no one took that idea seriously.

Whether it was overfishing or another cause, the stocks of Pacific Northwest salmon, the Atlantic salmon, whatever salmon were in Europe, had all crashed at one time or another.

"We're the last fishing survivors," Reuben said. "We've been blessed with having such pristine habitat. We don't have that logging, the dams. Are we gonna be able to hold all that stuff off forever? I don't know."

Gease had joined us on the deck and he observed that king runs were down all over the state, not just in the Kenai River. The Anchor River, Kasilof River, the Little Susitna, all rivers normally graced with significant king populations, were also hurting. Gease believed the harsh winter may have affected everything.

"The runs may be late," Gease said. "That would be a good-case scenario. The bad case is that they're not there."

It was too soon to know which scenario would prove true for the Kenai. It was also too soon to tell what the long-term impact might be on guide businesses or for those who bought high-priced real estate on the shore of the river because of its bounty of fish. Reuben said he had not experienced a large number of cancellations by fishermen, and expected business would be better when coho fishing began in July.

I bumped into a couple in Anchorage that represented a different group of Kenai River users. Bud and Kathy Gabriel from Canby, Oregon, own a house on the river, at about mile 23, and they spend about ten weeks a year in Alaska. Their infatuation with Alaska began in 1990 and they visited regularly, often enough to convince them the way to go was to invest in their own property. "We love it," Bud Gabriel said. "There's no place like it."

They've become grand Alaska hosts. They invite friends and family from the Lower 48 to join them on the Kenai River all summer long to fish.

About four years ago they were red fishing and saw a huge gray tail poke out of the water. A hard-pulling king grabbed the hook, but they lost the fifty pounder at the boat. It was reeled all of the way in, but spit the hook. "We prayed that morning for a big fish," Bud said.

It turned out a big king had Kathy's name on it within 300 yards of their house. She was admiring the scenery, admittedly not devoting 100 percent attention to her rod when a fish swallowed the hook and yanked the rod downward. "I'm never ready," she said of being surprised by the development.

Kathy grabbed the rod and began reeling. Bud offered advice and instruction on how to reel in a big one. "Always obey the captain," Kathy said. The tug-of-war went on and she felt the strain in her arms. "Of course I was tired, but time flies when you're having fun," she said.

And it's difficult to have more fun on the water than bringing in a sixty-eight-pound king—especially when you have a mount made to preserve the memory.

Bud admitted to concern over the poor king salmon run to start the 2012 season, but was hopeful it would be a temporary condition. As an Oregon fisherman he was well versed in the ups and downs of salmon history on the Columbia River. "We have seen enough of a salmon comeback in Oregon to know that they can come back," he said.

RIDING THE RIVER

Gary Galbraith is the raft man. He owns Alaska Rivers Company and since 1976 has been guiding rafting trips on the Kenai River, the Upper River, where no motors are allowed. For a quarter of a century I have been taking the peaceful raft journeys with Gary with various members of my family. I have also recommended the trip to every single tourist I know who visits Alaska. But this late June journey was my first trip in some years and the first one with grandchildren, the youngest of whom was just old enough to float the river. This was the first of a couple of planned Kenai family visits with school out of session for the summer.

Gary is sixty-one now and he long ago committed to his place in the woods overlooking the river as his piece of paradise. After decades of skiing, mountain climbing, rafting, paddling, and guiding he has purposely slowed down and become more or less a one-step-removed executive. He has turned over almost all operational functions of the rafting business to hired assistants. Only when he feels like it does he guide anymore. So having him as our guide for the two-and-half-hour trip on the river pretty much amounted to special Alaska Rivers treatment out of friendship.

His hair is grayer than it used to be (Whose isn't?), but his enthusiasm is the same as ever. "The only people that I know that are getting old are the people around me," Galbraith said. "I have the best job in the world. I've always loved the river. I'm kind of a greeter."

Gary is not particularly tall, five-nine-ish, but he has broad shoulders and powerful arms and I always marveled at how he could power the raft downriver on muscles only. He has owned this business a long time, and while he delegates to twenty-somethings and high school kids working their first jobs, he is still the general overseer. "It owns me," he joked about the company.

Gary is definitely not sitting around in a rocking chair. He skis an exceptional amount in the winter. He used to run a charter boat out of Seward that he took out on Resurrection Bay and he still has it, but now he uses it only for pleasure fishing, not taking clients out. He is on a second marriage (been married to Yvette for six years), with some younger kids (boys sixteen and thirteen) added to the mix. His first wife and one of his sons were killed in an automobile accident years ago while another son grew up on the riverfront property. He is now thirty and is a civil engineer in Anchorage. Gary doesn't live in the large house adjacent to the river now, but the land, the trees, the buildings that he built, are all part of him.

"My family was born here," Gary said of his first family. "I've got my family's ashes here. My ashes will be, too, unless they can stuff me."

Guide work on the water has been in the Galbraith family for three generations. A grandfather was a fishing guide in Minnesota. Gary's father ran charter boats in South Carolina. For Gary, the Kenai River was the place to be and although he is far from an every-day rafting guide now, he still likes to get out, needs to get out.

"If I couldn't be part of the river, I don't know," he said. "I couldn't imagine

Gary Galbraith has been guiding rafters and fishermen on the Kenai's Upper River since the 1970s and revels in the peace of that nonmotorized section of the river.

trying to start over doing something else. This is the most beautiful place in the world."

On this day the Alaska Rivers Company grounds were jammed with people, perhaps fifty signed up for rafting trips. Some years ago Gary signed a deal with a local hotel to offer rafting as an entertainment option for tourists and that has been a boon. There was a big group from the hotel readying to set off on a wild Alaska river.

Brown bears, moose, eagles, all kinds of fish, the wildlife in this little corner of the Kenai, are difficult to catalog and count. "Oh, there's a bear over there in the trees," Galbraith said matter-of-factly. Several heads swiveled. It was a prop, a stuffed bear.

"I didn't say what kind of bear," Gary said as he laughed.

My daughter Alison, grandsons Malachi, going on eleven, and Britain, going on six, and I, piled into the raft bobbing on the Kenai. Gary climbed in behind us and flexing his arm muscles grabbed hold of the oars and shoved off into the current. When we informed Britain that we were going rafting, he informed us he didn't know what a raft was.

We adults in the family were trying to give the boys an appreciation of the Alaska outdoors and just how special the Kenai River was. Malachi took one look at the swirling waters, as benign as they really were, and said, "It looks scary." Britain, who was trying to be open-minded about the experience said, "If we went fast it would freak us out."

We all wore life jackets and most of us took advantage of the offering of rubber boots to keep feet warm and dry. Alison made the choice of sticking with Crocs on her feet, which meant that they did get cold and wet.

Since we were not fishing we were not going to see sockeye or silver salmon, Dolly Varden or rainbow trout. We hoped to spot a bear from a safe distance, a moose crashing through the trees, or an eagle soaring overhead. Some years ago, while Gary and I were talking in his yard we were interrupted by two eagles engaged in combat in the air above us. It was a sight to see.

Gary reassured the nervous boys that the river was safe and that no one had ever fallen out of any of his rafts. It was quiet on the river. The only noise was the dipping of the oars in the water and then, as we came around a bend, the mini-roar of some small rapids that foamed white, but were not rough at all. Almost as soon as we started downriver, Gary pointed out an eagle. It was perched in a nest in a tree.

Gary rowed in the back, I sat in the middle, Alison and the boys sat closer to the front. "How are we doing up there, gang?" Gary asked. Britain said he was fine. Malachi didn't answer. He seemed nervous. Gary said he now personally only took out fishing families with kids, letting other guides do the work with those more competitive fishermen likely to focus on the catch more than the relaxation.

I had taken this same rafting journey many times with Gary. I found it peaceful, pleasurable, a tangible connection to the Alaska wilderness, drinking in the sights of the Kenai. Alison had been on the raft trip when she was much younger. I hoped the outdoors message, the nature connection, would grab the boys, make them want to do more things like this, be out as often as they could when they got older and made their own decisions.

Everything was slightly off-kilter during this season on the Kenai with the kings not showing up in force and the reaction to the record snows of winter, and this raft guide noticed differences in the river, too. "Look at how high the water is," Gary pointed out. "We had so much snowfall. It's definitely more turbid than it usually is."

Apparently now convinced that we were not going to capsize, Malachi moved around a bit on the raft and paid more attention to the scenery as the water flowed past the thick stands of trees and a group of harlequins. "I'm not worried anymore," he said. "It looks like everything is moving, but we're moving."

"Everything else is moving," I said to myself, "except time."

Harlequins are extremely colorful ducks. They have patches of gray and white and orange running along their sides and up onto their faces. "Duckies," Malachi said. "They're cute."

"That's the first brood I've seen this year," Galbraith said.

Rapids on the Kenai are baby rapids, not much more than a foot or so high. They interrupt the smooth flow of the river and don't last long, but they are visually arresting. "Uh, oh," Malachi said.

Gary teased the boys. "You want to go over the big water?" he said.

"Look at that big rock," Malachi said, pointing at a hunk of rock sticking up in the middle of the rapids where the water rushed around it. "I don't see any rock," Galbraith joked.

We crossed over the rapids with a mini-bump and by using his longstanding experience and some elbow grease, Galbraith steered the raft smoothly around the rock. "That was scary," Malachi said.

We pointed out a bird sitting in a tree to Britain. "What's that up there?" "Eagle," he said. The kid was learning.

Then we spied two more eagles. Unusual, Galbraith said, for two to hang out together the way these were. Far, far above us in the Kenai Mountains, Galbraith saw two white dots. He was the one with eagle eyes. Gary said the white spots were Dall sheep, but to me they could have been snow remnants.

Galbraith rowed us into the Russian River where the sockeye pour through. "I want to see fishies," Malachi said.

"We're gonna see a bazillion fish," Gary said. Maybe not that many, but just peering out of the raft down at the clearer water we could see flashes of red streaking past. "Watch out, one might jump in the boat. That would be fun."

Combining the current and Gary's workout, we were floating at between six and eight miles per hour. It was the middle of the week, during the middle of the day, and most people would probably be working. But hundreds of anglers lined the banks of the Russian, hungry to get in on the reds run. Near the raft a few reds jumped out of the water, clearing the surface by a foot, as if practicing for the high jump. "Whoa!" The startle factor was high.

To our left was a gathering of seagulls on a gravel bar. No dummies, they understood that free meals were available. Every time an angler cleaned a red salmon at one of the cutting tables the head and guts were tossed into the water. The gulls made a free-for-all charge after the extraneous pieces and filled their stomachs.

At the narrowest point in the Russian, two fishermen stood in the water, protected by waders, but including their casts they didn't leave much room for us to pass. Gary hailed them and warned them we were coming. "Usually, I knock 'em all down like bowling pins," Galbraith joked. We made it past the fishermen without an international incident.

In the old days of Galbraith's operation he used to slide the raft onto land midway through the trip and whip out a snack of chocolate chip cookies, reindeer sausage, cheese, and crackers. The goodies are still offered, but before the trip begins, while people are pulling on the life jackets and boots, and now he no longer pulls over for a mid-float pause. I was always very fond of those snacks. The taste of the reindeer sausage (which I have yet to encounter anywhere but Alaska) stayed with me a long time. Those cookies were darned good, too.

I will say that in those days when we pulled off the river into the trees, Galbraith always warned us about the possibility of a bear sneaking up on us, so it wasn't all that relaxing while we snacked. This represents one of those minor dilemmas of the wild in Alaska. You always want to have the experience of seeing the most exotic wildlife available, but you don't want to get attacked by it, either, whether it is a rowdy moose or a grumpy bear. It was always best to see the big critters from a distance when you had an escape route. This summer I was seeing eagles every time I drove to the Kenai and went out on the Kenai, but never ran into a bear.

One thing we saw a lot of were downed trees, trees blown over by high winds, trees tumbled at their roots where bank erosion spread. "They got chopped down," Britain announced, envisioning a Paul Bunyan lumberjack taking them out rather than Mother Nature.

Sure enough, more eagles. There were eagles everywhere. Two circled above. One flew past, its powerful wings flapping hard and propelling it forcefully. There were two more eagles in a tree. There was no mistaking them for another kind of bird. The white head was quite distinctive and the brown plumage was unmistakable. Seeing so many eagles was a reminder of what a comeback in nature they had made. The American bald eagle, the symbol of the country, the national bird (except maybe on Thanksgiving), was an endangered species in the second half of the twentieth century.

It would have been embarrassing for the national bird to go extinct, but in the 1950s it was estimated that there were only 412 nesting pairs remaining in the Lower 48. The pesticide DDT was blamed for much of the decline in the population of the majestic bird.

Public awareness and public education, as well as strict federal rules governing human contact with the bird, led to recovery and in 1995 the bald eagle was removed from the endangered species list. In 2007, it was removed from the threatened species list in the Lower 48. Along the Kenai River, it

Eagles seemed to be everywhere along the Kenai River all summer long in 2012. The national bird likes to eat salmon as much as the next fisherman.

seemed, eagles were as common as pigeons in a major, US industrialized city.

It was not as if you could readily see eagles everywhere in the Lower 48, but they were back at some strength in the places where you think you should see them, places such as wintering grounds on the Mississippi River on the border between Iowa and Illinois, and along the ocean coasts and other large bodies of water.

We kept seeing more eagles as we floated, a high count even by my summer standards. We saw more eagles than there are on the Philadelphia Eagles.

All too soon (we made fast time) the trip ended after eleven miles of river sightseeing. Galbraith guided the raft into Jim's Landing, a boat launch, preparatory to loading us all into a van that retraced our distance covered by river on the road.

Alison admitted that she had made a wardrobe misjudgment in choosing to wear pants that left her lower legs bare, and the Crocs, that left her feet unprotected. Galbraith bent over to touch one of her toes. "These are cold feet," he said. "Do you have feeling?"

"Oh yeah," Alison said. "They feel cold."

Back at Alaska Rivers Company, talk was of others seeing bears. Kyle, the older of Galbraith's stepsons, said his group spotted a brown bear with two cubs, and a black bear. "We saw the teddy bear, too (referring to the stuffed bear), so that means we saw five," he said.

The chief characteristic of the Upper River is the sound of silence. There are no roar of boat engines because there is no high-speed travel. Battles have been fought over the years to keep that section of the Kenai River free from motorized transport and Galbraith said his involvement in that fight is something he considers to be part of his legacy on the river.

"It's so nice without the noise," he said.

Galbraith looked around at the buildings he built, at the river flowing behind his land, his wife, his family, a new puppy being broken in, and yes, even that stuffed bear, and said, "This will always be home."

As for our boys, it wouldn't bother me one bit if someday they made a place along the Kenai River their home. This was a start. Now that the trip was over and they were off the river, nobody was nervous or scared. The "big waves" had become a favorite part of the float. They remembered them now as if they had been a carnival ride at the state fair.

EXCEPTION TO THE RULES

On the last day of the month, Mike and Murray Fenton of the Fenton Brothers Guide Service obtained a waiver from Alaska Fish and Game to take a very special customer fishing for king salmon on the Kenai River.

James, fourteen, a young man from Maine, had applied to the Make A Wish Foundation for the chance go fishing on Alaska's favorite river, if and when he was able during his months-long fight while trying to survive a brain tumor. For guys like James, Fish and Game can make an exception to the restrictive fishing rules.

After coping with the frightening initial diagnosis and enduring debilitating rounds of treatment, James's illness was in remission, the tumor had disappeared, and his future looked good. That all came after two surgeries and four stints of chemotherapy, some of which left him with blurred vision.

James, who comes from an outdoors oriented family, explained his choosing the Kenai River and king salmon for his wish boiled down to one of his aunts having a salmon mount on her wall. He said he also heard about the famed river from other fishermen.

Mike and Murray, who normally take different groups of clients out on the river, had the rare opportunity to spend time together in one of their boats. "I got to fish with my brother," Mike said of one of the highlights of the day. "We don't get to do that very often."

Technically speaking, neither Fenton brother actually fished. James's father, also named James, and his mother, Valerie, accompanied them, but the only person with a rod in the water was the younger James. Mike and Murray guided, provided light banter entertainment, and were there to pounce on a fish when James hooked one. Which he did. The youth, who had been unlucky enough to contract such a serious illness, had a lucky day of fishing.

James hooked two grown-up king salmon, one jack (a little one), and five rainbow trout during his outing, an exceptional day by any standard. James was able to use salmon eggs for bait, far more attractive to the fish than an empty hook, and he had the only line in the water as the Fentons moved the boat around to normally productive spots such as Big Eddy, College Hole, and Poachers Cove. Their knowledge, the bait availability, and James's persistence paid off.

The first king James landed was estimated at thirty-five pounds, a very respectable haul, and it involved considerable wrestling on the young angler's part. As it so happened that was the vamp till ready because the second king James hooked was a bigger one and involved more muscle to bring it to the boat. Mike Fenton guessed it weighed about fifty-five pounds and James couldn't even get his hands around the big, fat tail when the fish was released.

For the Fentons, in an otherwise gloomy summer, guiding James was a highlight. For James, the experience of catching many fish and big fish on the Kenai River could be summed up succinctly.

"It was amazing," he said.

Carlie Benefield had a blast at the Kenai River Junior Classic for kids. She was totally into the spirit of the occasion, including kissing her fish for luck when she caught it.

July

IN CASE OF EMERGENCY

The worst damage I have ever done to myself fishing on the Kenai is piercing a finger with a hook and drawing a trickle of blood. I did have a good friend, however, who cast in an awkward motion and hooked himself in the back of the head. Not only did it hurt like the devil, he couldn't see the wound, and worse, the hook stuck in his noggin and he could do nothing on his own to remove it.

When you do something like that you feel like a dork. But you're stuck, in more ways than one. So John had to quell his embarrassment and trek to Central Peninsula Hospital in Soldotna for emergency action. They are used to walk-ins like that at this particular hospital. Over the course of the summer, for decades now, fishermen in pain show up at the emergency room door gushing blood or showing off grisly penetrations in their bodies. The stories may be funny in the telling, and the victims may be forevermore sheepish about what happened, but sometimes there is nothing to laugh about at all.

The incidence of wounded-by-hook human reached such a crescendo in the 1980s that the hospital began saving the weapons causing the damage and displaying them. A mannequin was posted near the emergency room and every time a doctor or nurse extricated a wicked sharp hook from flesh it was inserted into the same place on the mannequin to represent the spot of injury. By the end of the fishing season the mannequin was typically decorated by so much metal it would never have been able to be taken through an airport detector.

More recently the mannequin was replaced by non–3-D cloth wall hangings of a man and a woman. They resembled cloth dolls that a youngster might carry, except they were pretty flat. Although it was about six weeks or so into the fishing season, the caricatures were remarkably free of hooks. Three were inserted onto the man hanging and only one on the woman. I wondered if this meant anglers were getting smarter and more careful in their casting, but the nurse on the scene would not offer such credit to the human race. She chalked up the low number of injured fishermen to date in the spring and early summer of 2012 to the absence of kings. There was a hidden benefit of a shortage of king salmon: fewer angler injuries.

One overall trend that has been noted by hospital personnel in recent years has been a decline in the number of eye injuries. Even among fishermen who don't ordinarily wear glasses consciousness-raising has prompted the wearing of protective goggles a la Kareem Abdul-Jabbar. Also, wearing hats helps protect eyes by deflecting flying hooks. It is difficult to imagine a more stomach-churning injury than taking a sharp hook in the eye. Still, emergency room personnel have not forgotten the time a nun came in hooked in the eye—she lost the eye.

"Maybe the message is getting through," the nurse said of anglers being more careful. But it also might not matter that much because "you never know who you're standing next to."

In that sense combat fishing is probably a bit like driving. You can stop at all of the stop signs or red lights and still get rear-ended.

People get hooked in the head, in the neck, in the cheek. They get hooks caught on fingers, stuck halfway through thumbs. One woman was hooked through the lip into her teeth and was gushing blood. Her husband rushed her to the hospital and then *he* fainted in the parking lot. Hooks were made to pierce skin and stick once they get stuck, so removing them is a delicate matter. When a fish is hooked it may take pliers to yank the hook from lips. That doesn't appeal to people when they are in a fix. They get squeamish about the idea of pulling a hook through their own flesh and often would rather consult professionals.

Reactions among those who show up at the hospital vary widely, sometimes because of the extent of the injury, and sometimes not. Some hooked anglers are horrified and can barely cope with the idea that the hook has penetrated skin so deeply it can't easily be removed. Others are more stoical. One fisherman showed up in the emergency room anxiously asking for a hook to be removed swiftly because the fish were running and he wanted to get back out on the river as fast as possible. He was told to calm down and reminded the emergency was what was happening to his body, not that he was missing out on fish.

Anyone who baits a hook is subject to sticking their fingers once in a while, but most of the time no major injury occurs from that. Likewise, halibut fishing in the sea at the edge of the Kenai Peninsula off of Homer doesn't produce much hook damage. King salmon fishing results in a little bit more, but the major culprit is sockeye fishing, particularly the combat fishing on the Russian River. That's where accidents happen most often. The anglers are almost elbow to elbow. The casts are more dramatic.

The hospital never has performed a scientific study about where hooks catch flesh most often or what the circumstances were. There are no charts or graphs with the info. Anecdotal evidence suggests that most hook injuries are self-inflicted. The most common fishing hook injuries are to the hands and the second most common are to the face and head. Apparently, a fisherman is the biggest menace to his own well-being, maybe more so than he is to the fish. But he still better watch out for his next-door fishing neighbor.

It's a bit macabre, but tourists who get wind of the replica man and woman on the wall do stop into the hospital emergency room to snap pictures. You can tell they're thinking, "Those crazy Alaskans." And when they bring the pix home and show them off to their friends, they probably start off by saying, "You're not going to believe this."

FISHING WITH THE FAM

On the day before daughter Alison and grandsons Malachi and Britain joined me on the Kenai River for an attempt to catch king salmon (even if we would

The emergency room at Central Peninsula Hospital in Soldotna is accustomed to anglers forced to make pit stops for medical treatment when they get hooked attempting to catch fish. These cloth human replicas hang on a wall and a hook is placed in the spot where a person was injured.

still have to release them) we stopped into the Soldotna Visitors Center to pay a visit to Les Anderson's record fish and another huge king that is the second largest ever caught on rod and reel.

This fish was caught by Pat Plautz on the Kenai River on July 17, 1990, and weighed ninety-five pounds, ten ounces. The fish was displayed in a glass case on the floor and so our littlest guy, Britain, lay down on the floor next to it to see how he measured up. Britain weighed forty-eight pounds at that time as he approached his sixth birthday. Malachi, his older brother, guessed his own weight as eighty-something pounds. All of this means the fish was much bigger than either of the kids.

"What do you think of that fish?" I asked Britain.

"It's crazy," he said.

Good observation, actually. I glanced at Malachi and said, "Now you know what your goal is for tomorrow." He was skeptical. "Oh, no, I'm not catching a fish that big," he said. I turned back to Britain. "Are you going to catch a fish bigger than you? I don't think you could." He was bolder. "Yeah, I could."

Plautz's brother Gary was a guide for RW's Fishing & Big Eddy Resort, located adjacent to the Harry Gaines fish camp and the Plautzes were fishing over the lunch hour at Sunken Island when Pat, who is from Oregon, hooked the gigantic, thrashing king salmon in just three-and-a-half feet of water.

"It took twenty minutes to land," said resort owner R. W. Weilbacher who goes by RW. "He grew up fishing salmon his whole life." But Plautz hadn't seen a salmon like this before—few ever have.

RW was so thrilled by the big catch that he had a skin mount made and gave it to Plautz, but he also had more than one fiberglass mount made. One is the replica on display at the Visitors Center. Another remains hanging in RW's living room at the resort.

"It was the catch of a lifetime," RW said. "I've been trying to beat it ever since."

Plautz did not return to fish for king salmon again for three years (probably thinking he had a tough act to follow, so why bother), RW said. "He caught some kings. But then he went halibut fishing and caught a 312-pound halibut." A halibut that size is a trophy, and for most people would also be a catch of a lifetime. "And he hasn't been back since," RW said. Plautz probably felt he had conquered all that Alaska had to offer.

I was not really anticipating a ninety-five-pound, ten-ounce fish being nabbed by Malachi. The first time Malachi went fishing he was five years old and I brought him to a backyard pond owned by a friend in a Chicago suburb. A few of my friends were there, too, so he had adult supervision. I wanted him to like the experience, build an interest in fishing and the outdoors, and catch some fish. I was worried because he was Mr. Impatience and one key element of fishing is having patience. There's no way to know if fish will bite on a given day even if you have fished in the same place before and know it as a hot spot.

There was no need to worry. On this day the pond was quite generous. Malachi caught and released twenty bluegill in forty-five minutes. It was astounding. He was using a kid's Superman rod and he was reeling them in as if there was no tomorrow. When we drove away from the pond he said, "Can we go again tomorrow?" That's what you want to hear.

Another time Britain, who was just a baby at the time, joined us at the same pond. He caught the first fish of his life—a bluegill—sitting on his mother's lap on a bench on the dock overlooking the pond. He did some reeling, but the real work was done by Alison.

A few years before this Kenai sojourn, Malachi got his baptism on the Kenai River. He, his mom, and I ventured out with one of Reuben Hanke's guides. The night before that trip I thumbed through the Alaska Fish and Game regulations to make sure the eight-year-old didn't need a fishing license. Nope, he was home free. But the cover of the annual magazine-like rule booklet featured a picture of a little boy holding a silver salmon in his arms. I showed Malachi the picture and said, "That's you tomorrow."

Malachi loved it when the boat picked up speed and the wind parted his hair. Just loved it when we were going fast.

"This is the best day of my life!" he announced. OK, if you say so. When the boat was parked and the fish were ignoring us he got bored. "This is the worst day of my life," he said. Well, easy come, easy go. Clearly, he was comparing coho salmon fishing to bluegill fishing.

After the mood swings, however, Malachi caught a silver salmon and although he didn't offer the same embrace as the boy in the picture, the net effect was the same. The only help he got from me reeling it into the boat was the occasional finger under the front of the rod pushing it higher in the air. Otherwise he brought in a seven-pound silver by his lonesome. He didn't want to touch its icky skin, in his words, especially with a trail of blood coming out of the fish's mouth, and the guide dropped it into the fish box in the back of the boat.

A little while later, with no other action going on, Malachi asked if he could look at his fish. Certainly, I said, and he and I took the few steps to the rear of the boat and I flipped open the top of the fish box. As he leaned forward for a close-up look at his fish, he got a shock. The fish started flapping and squirming. Malachi had expected a limp, dead fish. As far as he could tell, this fish was haunted. When the fish shook, Malachi screamed and jumped in the air. I thought his vertical leap could have matched LeBron James at that moment. I burst into laughter, guffawing so loudly I fell to my knees. If Malachi had jumped any higher from fright we would have had a man overboard incident.

Now we were back for another try, with both boys, little brother going out salmon fishing for the first time after his introduction to the river on a raft a few weeks earlier. Our guide was Cody Dutcher, the same young man who took me out with the more experienced fisherman, twelve-year-old Ryan.

It was overcast and once again fairly cool for a midsummer's morning, with temperatures in the thirties. I only hoped it didn't rain. That could really put the kids into a foul mood. As it was, we were tempting fate. Over a period of a few years Malachi was going from fishing for the sure-thing bluegill, to the pretty available coho salmon, to chasing king salmon during a time when catching one would pretty much classify as a mini-miracle.

Still, we had booked the trip, some fish were in the Kenai, and we weren't going to get one of the rare beauties by sitting on shore. At the least young Malachi would learn that fishing and catching are not synonyms. Into every growing up a little innocence must be lost and a little reality dosage must be applied. No one catches king salmon every time they fish. Remember those Fish and Game statistics about it taking an average of forty-two hours to catch one even with a guide? But I was hoping for them more than they were hoping for themselves as we shoved off from the dock at the Harry Gaines fish camp.

There were four seats in the boat besides the guide seat, so we were spread out and holding on tight as we zoomed off to find a good fishing spot on the overcast morning. We created our own wind and the engine made too much noise to talk until we halted.

"Momma, that was freaking me out," Britain asserted about our speed. Malachi felt differently. "Awesome!" he declared.

Rods out, waiting for a bite, we contemplated the river and the situation requiring patience to see a king salmon. But kids' minds didn't go on hold. "What if a fish jumped into the boat and you grabbed it," Malachi said to Alison. "Then I would be really lucky," she said.

There was a decent smattering of boats out on the water carrying hopeful fishermen. As of July 1 the regulation demanding catch and release had eased, although the regulation banning the use of bait was still in effect. This was no kids' fishery like the bluegill pond. This was hard fishing seeking rare fish and there was competition from other fishermen.

"Have you ever caught anything, Alison?" Cody asked. "I've never caught anything," she said.

This needed slight amplification. Alison had never caught anything on the Kenai River, in probably three tries, but she had caught halibut out of Homer, so she wasn't a complete Alaska fishing novice. "I snagged a humpy once in

Valdez," she proclaimed after another minute of thinking about her minimal fishing past.

A slew of boats sought well-known hot spots, so we were hemmed in sometimes when Cody moved the boat around angling for position. It was almost combat fishing by boat, it was so tight at times.

"Are there any crocodiles?" Malachi blurted out.

Crocodiles on the Kenai. That's rich. Malachi does not troll the Internet, but the timing of his interrogatory was interesting. Only the day before there had been a story making the rounds online about a gigantic, twenty-foot-plus-long croc that weighed about 2,000 pounds being certified as a *Guinness World Records* record.

The river was swollen. You could tell by how it slopped over the banks in certain places, with small trees poking through the surface. The snowmelt did make a difference in the depth and width of the Kenai. We were facing pretty murky water, making it hard for whatever kings were around to see the hooks.

"She's a big thing this year," Cody said. "Now if it will only clear in the next couple of days."

It was a bit surprising to see how many fishermen took their dogs out on a boat with them. They had to be well-behaved and not jump around and yip when a fish was caught and they had to be smart enough not to step too close to the edge of the boat. We saw one dog wearing a life jacket and Britain loved that. It seemed cartoonish to him.

"He has a doggy life jacket," Britain announced. "It's a person life jacket."

We came upon such sights a bit less frequently than Britain would have enjoyed since we had no activity that involved a fishing rod. "Fishing is all about waiting," Alison informed him. Right about that, kids. Only an hour into the scheduled six-hour fishing trip, Britain inquired if he were finished yet. "I'm bored," he said.

"You can swim back to Harry Gaines fish camp," Cody said.

The sun began peeking through the clouds. That was always a welcome sign because an appearance by the sun cooked the chill out of the air and provided more comfort. A typical side effect of the snowmelt running into the river was also a notable amount of tree branches floating past. Some of the junk was pretty large, like logs that were not big enough to threaten us, but were big enough to make a good bang if we hit.

"I feel like every log in the river is coming at my boat," Cody said.

For amusement, Alison and Britain counted logs as they swirled our way. They were up to four. That was actually a lot. Many days you could fish for hours and never see one.

Out of nowhere Britain expressed concern that we might catch and eat Nemo. Nemo? The name sounded familiar, but I wasn't up on my kids animated movies. All I knew was that Nemo was some kind of cartoon fish. Nemo was a fake clownfish, it turns out. No worries, Britain.

As hard as it was to find king salmon, it was once again remarkably easy to spot bald eagles. They were everywhere. Some were soloists and once we saw a group of six or seven together on the shore. Pretty outstanding stuff on loan from nature there. For a moment, a couple of hours into the morning, we felt a few light drops of rain. Oh, boy, the kids would hate that. Luckily, the wet stuff halted quickly without really wetting us.

"Which way is the North Pole?" Britain asked.

Uh, north. He wanted to embark on a road trip to the North Pole to see Santa Claus and his "purple" reindeer. That would have to wait until another day.

We hunkered down as Cody motored to another spot in search of the fish. Malachi rode with his hood off, head turned into the wind, which was strong enough and cold enough to seemingly distort his face, as if he was in his own cartoon. He also dipped his hand into the water to test the temperature and was shocked by how cold it felt. The air temperature was in the forties, the sun wasn't warming the water, so it was possibly in the thirties.

"We were going across like a skipping stone," he said, which was a pretty cool description of cruising over the water at a certain speed.

After dropping our hooks into the water at the new place and waiting for another decent interval, Malachi asked a perfectly reasonable question. "I wonder where all the fish are?" he said.

"In the water," I replied.

"Not here," he said.

"They're swimming all around your hook," I said.

"They're missing your hook, too," he said. Touché.

"When are you guys gonna catch fish?" Britain chimed in, as if he wasn't really part of this catching expedition. "Good question," I said. "We need to check with other professionals."

"Like him," Britain said, pointing at Cody.

"Like god," I added.

Somehow talk turned to the banana superstition. None of us were guilty of including a banana with breakfast. Cody was a banana superstition acolyte. "If there's a banana on the counter, I don't even look at it," he said. "It's like a hornet's nest. You might not get stung, but why take the chance?"

In the days leading up to this excursion, much energy was expended discussing how neat it would be to catch a big, meaty king salmon. As the clock ticked down on the morning, Malachi lowered his sights.

"I don't care if it's small," he said. "I just want to catch a fish."

Guides on the Kenai River sometimes converse with one another by radio, especially guides who work for the same service, or who are friends. They may offer tips on where the fish are biting and they try to help out buddies having a tough time. Cody was on the radio with another guide and we heard him say, "I haven't had anything today. I can't even get a sockeye today."

That gloomy and accurate report was not going to gain us any instant company from Cody's pals shifting locations to join us. "I know of one king lost," Cody said. "A couple of others were caught."

In Anchorage, there is a well-known market called New Sagaya that specializes in fresh Alaskan seafood. Grasping the concept of getting skunked, Malachi advanced the idea that if we really wanted salmon we should make a detour on the way home.

"We should just go to New Sagaya and buy salmon and tell people we caught it," he said.

He apparently didn't quite grasp the idea that was not kosher behavior.

As Cody maneuvered the boat to shore next to fish camp, with us fishless, Britain announced, "No fish caught today." Bingo. "They go to New Sagaya to die." Cracked me up. It was sad, but true.

Later, as he ate a plate of waffles with maple syrup for dinner, our little philosopher said, "We would be eating fish for dinner if we caught one."

THE KENAI RIVER CLASSIC

A few dozen hopeful anglers, guides, and government officials stood in Bob Penney's large driveway before sitting down to an outdoor salmon dinner under a canopy. For once, the buzz before the annual Kenai River Classic contained as much concern as lighthearted commentary, though the two sentiments did mix.

On the eve of the nineteenth annual event created to draw attention to the river and raise money for restoration and habitat conservation, organizers had to wonder if anyone would actually catch a king salmon in the Kenai over the next couple of days of fishing.

The entire reason this event began was to help prevent a day like this coming. The Classic attracted the rich and the governmentally powerful for a good time, but most importantly in the mind of Penney, who was one of the main initiators of the event, it was designed to educate the movers and shakers with the power to pass the laws that could affect the Kenai River.

The concept, hatched with the late US Senator Ted Stevens, was based on the theory, "If you see it, you will love it." But even more important than that, it was a hopeful case of if you see it, you will understand it, and understand why it is imperative that its wildness be preserved.

There were many serious faces in the gathering worrying about the king salmon shortage, but there was also gallows humor. Congressman Don Young, Alaska's only member of the US House of Representatives because of its small population, cracked a joke in the middle of the discussion of how tough it would be to catch a king this time.

"So what else is new?" said Young, disparaging his own fishing prowess.

One of the welcoming speakers was Mark Hamilton. Hamilton, a retired US Army major general and the retired president of the University of Alaska system, promptly bought a house on the Kenai River when he stepped down from his educational position in 2010. He was helping with the Classic. Hamilton commented that everyone there loved the Kenai River, but "Now this river needs some love back."

US Senator Mark Begich praised Penney for his long-term efforts to aid the river and said that early on in his term he had a scheduled appointment at the *Peninsula Clarion*, the local daily paper, and Penney offered to pick him up at the airport and drive him. It is basically a five-minute ride from point A to point B, but seizing the opportunity Penney held Begich more or less captive, taking the time to educate him about the Kenai River's status and needs.

"Thirty minutes later I realized we'd driven past the *Clarion* building six times," Begich said.

Considerable credit for getting the Classic up and running and attracting influential Washington politicians to the Kenai River for a getaway goes to Ted Stevens. "Without Ted's participation and leadership, we would never have gotten it going," Penney said.

Penney, Stevens, and Ben Ellis, who at the time was executive director of the Kenai River Sportfishing Association, were fishing one day and they started brainstorming about fund-raising. Somebody mentioned that in the Lower 48 there were all of these charitable golf tournaments held.

Penney appealed to Stevens, who was one of the most powerful men in the Senate, and was known for the way he was able to steer various financial benefits to Alaska through his influence. "What can we do?" Penney asked. "They (golf events) raise all of this money for health issues. We need that. We need to protect this river. It's on the road system. It's the only red salmon fishery the public can get to in the United States because it's on the road system and it gets a lot of impact." Stevens said, "You know, if you guys got a sportfishing tournament going in July I could get some people to come up, some senators to come up."

The first year, in 1994, it cost $45,000 (invested by Penney) to put the tournament on and it returned $110,000, with entry fees of $3,000. Penney holds the kickoff dinner each year. Other sponsors have stepped up. Stevens fished every year until he died in a plane crash in 2010 at age eighty-six and he made sure the Kenai River became a well-known fishing hole to some of the nation's most important politicians. Celebrities from different walks of life also signed up.

Denny Crum, the retired Louisville college basketball coach, who won two NCAA titles, is an Alaskan devotee who has fished in the state for forty-four years in a row. He was also entered in the Classic about ten years in a row.

"That Classic was a fun event," Crum said. "You couldn't always predict what the weather would be, but that's how I got involved in fishing on the Kenai River. If you like salmon fishing there isn't a better place."

One year Crum won the tournament by catching a king salmon weighing sixty-one pounds.

In 2012, the entrants in the tournament would be able to keep a large king like that. Organizers scrupulously noted that everyone had the right to do so, but the subtle and not-so-subtle pressure leaned toward releasing anything caught and everyone got that message before the fishing began.

"We're up to a $4,000 entry fee now and it's still a pretty doggone good buy," Penney said. The 100-some-odd entrants received the pre-fishing dinner, two days of guided fishing in twenty-six boats on the Kenai, took away some salmon (reds), even if they didn't catch them, and received a plaque of gratitude for helping the river. Also covered by the fee were two days of lodging, all other meals, entertainment, a gear bag, and transportation. The cost of hosting one person runs between $2,500 and $3,000 and the remainder goes to funding the Sportfishing Association, according to Gease. The fee is a tax-deductible donation, he said.

Unlike the old days, when Stevens played a large role in rounding up contestants, the Classic has evolved into more of an Alaskan event. There are still politicians and others from Outside, but the majority of government officials are legislators from in-state now.

"It's not like a bass tournament where you get money," Penney said. "You get recognition for what you've done. But the money goes back to habitat preservation. So Ted Stevens was the catalyst that allowed us to grow the Kenai River Classic in which we raise money to be able to have a full-time staff and a full-time office. He's really the one who helped us to raise the money to put back into the habitat. We're very proud of what we've done."

As expected, and as warned, fishing was slow during the Classic. Just eight kings were caught and everyone released theirs. The biggest fish was caught by Súsie Ellis, Ben's wife, a forty-two incher. The second biggest fish was caught by Dan Saddler, an Alaska state representative from Eagle River, near Anchorage, and a one-time journalism colleague of Ellis's with the defunct *Anchorage Times*. He came close to the title, with a forty-one-inch fish.

"We shipped everybody ten pounds of sockeye salmon," Ricky Gease said. "It was very much an educational event."

The circumstances of catch and release and the general knowledge that fish were not returning to the river in huge numbers made for a different kind of Classic. As there was everywhere else where fishermen and fish experts gathered for any length of time during the summer of 2012, much speculation was advanced on the why of the missing salmon.

"A lot of it is trying to figure out why the ocean, for whatever reason, is not being productive," Gease said. "There are more fish coming into the river now than there were, but we're not likely to meet the escapement. It's now around 500 a day and they need 1,000 a day to meet the escapement. It's just weird. There are unusual weather patterns."

Pretty soon the pinks, or humpies, would arrive, pouring into the Kenai by the thousands and in their own way confusing the fishery. No one seemed to appreciate those salmon, but Gease said he had been hearing from his Kenaitze Indian Tribe wife, Clare Swan, passing on the message of his eighty-two-year-old mother-in-law elder that people shouldn't look down on them. One day, she said, that might be all you have to eat.

Or they might be the only salmon to fish for. I knew exactly what she meant. Catching humpies could be a lot of fun, but they did need a public relations agent to beef up their image among guides. Guides had to stop badmouthing them as being a nuisance interfering with the catch of king salmon or silver salmon and talk them up as an action fishery in their own right.

Somewhat coincidental to the timing of the Classic, I was reading a book called *Early Warming* by prominent Alaskan author Nancy Lord. It dealt with climate change in the North, but in part touched upon what might be happening in the oceans.

"Ocean temperatures may be a better indicator of global warming than air temperatures, because the ocean stores more heat and responds more slowly to change," she wrote. . . . "There are many other implications of climate change for our oceans, poorly understood at present. A warmer ocean will hold less oxygen, for one thing. . . . The danger of this acidification is that marine organisms have evolved to thrive within certain pH ranges, and the abrupt change in chemistry will stress them in ways only now suggesting themselves." Lord quoted an expert in ocean science from the University of Alaska Fairbanks as saying, "Alaska will be ground zero for ocean acidification, just as it is for climate change. Everywhere we look in Alaska we're finding areas that are already corrosive."

This is an extreme abridgement of Lord's work, but it may be supplying the answer to what's going wrong in the ocean that affects the food chain that in turn affects the salmon and has resulted in lower returns. Again, no one can be certain, but this is ominous information.

The Classic always concludes at the Harry Gaines fish camp. Reuben Hanke lends his dock and the land to the event. Over the years, as he has gained experience and become more aware of all the issues, he has become more active politically. In past years he always rented a booth at the Sportsman Show in April, but for the last two years he had been absent, his time spent in Juneau for a chunk of the legislative session, working as a lobbyist on river issues along with Gease.

"They only caught eight kings," Reuben said of the entrants in the Classic, "and some sockeye. It was upbeat, anyway. We filled twenty-six boats for two days. It's all for the river and all for the kings. We need these people now more than ever. They get it. And we need them to get it."

Since the establishment of the Kenai River Classic in 1994, its success and growth, the Kenai River Sportfishing Association has built upon the enthusiasm and added two more events to its annual summer cycle of fund-raising, events that provide education aimed at additional groups. In August of each year there is now a Kids Classic. In September, there is a Women's Classic.

None of these events is in jeopardy, but putting their planning where their philosophy is, and reacting to the low king return of 2012, the association is looking at a major shift in the dates the Classic is held from its perennial spot in early July to a likely calendar spot in August. The harsh reality of the poor king return, and the unknowns surrounding its future, are leading the association to pick a Classic date where the entrants will fish for coho, or silver salmon, instead of kings.

SUBSISTENCE FISHING

Alaska Fish and Game calls it "personal use" fishing. Everyone else in Alaska calls it subsistence fishing. This is Everyman fishing, not for sport, but definitely for food. At select times bodies of water are opened only to Alaska residents to dipnet. This has nothing to do with sportfishing, which by including the use of the word *sport* in its description implies fun fishing.

And this has nothing to do with commercial fishing, a profession that focuses on casting big nets into the water to haul in fish after fish to sell.

Subsistence fishing is fishing to subsist, to bring home fish to store in the freezer, to provide meals in the coming months. Dipnetting is not catching salmon one at a time on a hook with the use of an ounce of bait. Dipnetting may require a license, but there is no hiring of guides and most of the fish are taken from shore. If you do not live in the state you are not invited. This is Alaska-only fishing, the use of the resource by people who are the taxpayers.

Under Alaska rules, the head of a household can catch twenty-five salmon with a dip net and ten salmon for every other member of the household. The season is a short one on the Kenai River and in 2012 it was open from July 10 to July 31. Go get those sockeye, people! My friend Brian Walker of Anchorage makes an annual pilgrimage to the Kenai for red salmon. His twenty-one-year-old daughter, Jill, sat this one out, but his sons, Brian Jr., eighteen, and Simon, fifteen, joined him in the push for salmon. I went along as an observer.

Brian, forty-eight, is a big man. For several years he was a medal winner in strength events at the World Eskimo-Indian Olympics, the annual summer gathering in Fairbanks in which Alaska natives compete in a wide variety of indigenous games. He regularly won awards in the stick pull, Eskimo stick pull, and four-man carry. At about six-foot-two and weighing in the 280s or so, Walker had the build of a defensive tackle. His sons take after him and are also growing into big dudes.

Walker, who is part Athabascan Indian, said he believes that portion of his heritage has given him a taste for king salmon.

"A lot of people swear by Yukon River kings," Walker said of the pulsating great river that crosses Alaska's Interior and is a very productive fishery. "I love king salmon, but I think they taste different in different places."

Walker does not own a boat and that means he and his sons must fish from shore to obtain their red salmon. This is not rod and reel fishing as most people envision. Dipnetting is accomplished with a long-handled net that has a very large mouth. The best place for the Everyman to try to stock up on reds on the Kenai is to approach the river from Kalifornsky Beach. Access to the beach along the river is a mile or so from the road, though, and the soft sand does not welcome small vehicles or ones not equipped with

Anytime a fisherman brought his dip-net catch to shore to clean, a gaggle of seagulls surrounded him, waiting for the fish leavings to be thrown their way.

four-wheel drive. We all piled into Walker's Dodge truck for the slow drive through the sand to a parking place perhaps fifty yards from the water.

We did not pick a nice day for this outing. It was damp, periodically raining, with a strong wind blowing in. About two dozen trucks dotted the sand, their owners wearing layers to protect against the unseasonable chill (although there can be a chill on any given day in Southcentral Alaska).

Walker stepped out of the truck and said, "Smell the fish, guys?" to his sons. "Smells delicious," said son Simon.

The smell of fish was strong in the air, even with the breeze. When a dipnetter gathered in a salmon he walked it onto shore, dumped the fish out, and cleaned it. Off with its head, out with its guts. Those fish remainders were tossed aside and instantly were set upon by a flock of aggressive seagulls. A feeding frenzy ensued on the beach any time a fisherman went to work with his knife. The seagulls knew this dance, understood the procedure, but there might be fifty together seeking a small scrap of food, so they were in competition. As more and more fish were cleaned and the leavings were thrown aside, the birds became bolder, flying closer and closer to the fishermen. One group of gulls buzzed so closely around an angler that he

For three weeks in July, under Fish and Game regulations, Alaska residents are allowed to dipnet for red salmon for subsistence, or personal use. Here Brian Walker of Eagle River walks along the shore of the Kenai River carrying his long-handled net.

became irritated and threw a rock at them. That very much annoyed Walker. He scowled. "He's being mean to the seagulls."

The three Walkers, wearing chest waders, readied themselves for work. For work it is to dipnet at Kalifornsky Beach. Catching salmon takes effort. Each of them held one of the nets, with its sixty-inch spread in the nylon. The dipnetting pattern in this spot is peculiar to the area. Rather than a combat fishing scenario, there is a Kenai Walk performance, a march of sorts along the shore in water a couple of feet deep. The fishermen, each carrying a net, walk single file parallel to land over a distance of perhaps 100 yards, dragging the net under the surf. The idea is that salmon will swim into the net and be trapped, then carried out of the water and dissected.

"You keep your net parallel to the net frame so once they get in they can't get out," Walker said. "Hopefully, you get four or five fish."

Hopefully. Fish were being caught, not at a rapid rate, more like one at a time. As anyone who has walked in water can tell you, it takes a lot of work to lift your feet and make progress. It's harder yet when you are weighted down by waders, the water is waist deep, and you are dragging a net under the surface. Back and forth the fishermen walked, fighting the swirling water, which sometimes hit them with a wave, the wind, and the spitting rain. They allowed a decent interval between one another, but kept on trekking, usually withdrawing from the line only when they caught a fish. Or sometimes just to take a break from the challenge.

"I'll go out when I get tired," Walker said.

Brian Jr. trudged bare armed, oblivious to the cold. He was a true Alaskan. His arms and hands turned red, but he pooh-poohed it, saying the air and wetness didn't bother him. Simon, meanwhile, did get chilled and retreated to the truck where he turned on the engine and the heat for a bit.

On this day the red salmon were being almost as elusive as the kings. Brian walked back and forth, but his net came out of the water empty. Others nearby were catching fish and fending off seagulls, but they weren't hauling in reds in large numbers, several at a time, but one at a time.

Sockeyes are the favored eating fish by many. They are much smaller than kings, often seven pounds or so, but they are delectable, and this is the big opportunity to bring them home in large numbers. As is traditional, especially among native Alaska families, the bounty is not only for the immediate family. As the head of his four-person household, Walker's legal limit was fifty-five fish. But he planned to give some to neighbors, to elders who couldn't get out fishing for one reason or another, such as age or physical limitations. This is very much the role and tradition among the able-bodied in Alaska's small, remote villages where the trip to the river substitutes for the trip to the grocery store that doesn't exist in the first place.

"In this day and economy we're all a village," said Walker, who lives in the somewhat self-contained section of Anchorage called Eagle River.

The fish heads and guts were like a buffet table visit for the gulls. Since the catching wasn't as heavy as it sometimes is, the gulls had to be very aware of where the opportunity was. It was almost like the fish leavings resembled a loose football on the gridiron with someone shouting, "Fumble!" The entire pack of birds swooped down on the fish pieces en masse.

"When there is a lot of fish, it's a real killing field," Walker said.

Phil Cannon, thirty-six, a youth pastor from Anchorage, was doing the Kenai Walk in the line, too. He jokingly called it "water aerobics." Cannon made the 150-mile journey from the big city as part of a group of four and thought they had netted about a dozen red salmon.

"It's a fairly fruitful day," Cannon said. "They're [reds] my favorite. I fly fish for salmon on the Russian River. That's what I like." Cannon moved to Alaska from Michigan seven years earlier and he was mighty impressed by this kind of fishing roundup. "This is awesome stuff," he said. "It feels more like harvesting than fishing."

That was a fair description. It was working for your dinner instead of shopping for your dinner.

Daniel Pickett of Anchorage, an acquaintance of Walker's, and, as it turned out, a cousin of a friend of mine, was bundled up in a hood and gloves. He had taken a long leave of absence from dipnetting, about fifteen years, he said, and was making some headway, though this was nothing in comparison to the greatest dipnetting day of his life way back. He and his relatives harvested 150 reds in one day.

"This was work," Pickett said after carving up one salmon. "The Kenai River's an amazing system and it's known worldwide. It's just more complicated now. There are more people, more regulations than fifteen years ago."

The parade went on and on, fishermen doing their Kenai Walk in the water, hauling themselves out, walking back along the sand and then reentering the water. Brian Jr. seemed to work up a sweat. He rolled up the sleeves of his jersey. Brian Sr. took some breaks. The pace of fish being scooped into nets was discouraging. In the late afternoon, some people were quitting for the day, putting up tents, lighting fires.

"One thing about dipnetting," Walker said, "you're gonna get wet."

"My hands are freezing," Simon said.

Brian Jr. said it takes a lot more than this to freeze him out. He loves making these dipnetting trips and reminisced about the 2011 family outing when dad caught four squirming reds in one swipe of the net. Unlike the fella that threw a rock at the gulls swarming around his head, Brian Jr. had much more bird tolerance.

"They're not in the way," he said. "They know what we're doing."

Walker at last caught a salmon in his net and raised his arms in triumph. "First blood," he announced.

The fish was carried across the sand to an area by the truck and placed on a cutting board. Brian may only be eighteen, but he has been following dipnetting protocol for years. "Only all my life," he said. Slice, dice, the head was cut off, the salmon eggs excised from the belly. Brian brought the fish back to the water to wash off leftover mud from its body and in the seconds he was gone, all of us watching him, a gull zoomed in and grabbed the fish leavings from the board. Whoosh. This was getting to be more like *The Birds*, the Alfred Hitchcock movie, by the minute.

"It's a lot of work," Brian Sr. said. "A lot of cardio and leg work. It's tiring. I'm not going home till I get more fish. It's not a matter of them biting, it's a matter of them being there."

Bravado aside, fairly soon afterward the determination was made by Walker and the other fishermen that the reds weren't there in numbers at all. It made sense to rest and try again later when the tide came in, or the next day. Others scored better, but everyone knew more reds were going to pour into the Kenai River and there would be other days to fill their limits.

People who do not understand the challenges of actually catching twenty-five red salmon look at the rules and think it's a snap, that they can just go down to the beach, show up, and easily fill their nets and their freezers. That's an oversimplification. Some days, like this one, the fish win.

Don Hancock, who owns a sports card/memorabilia store in Anchorage, is the head of a household. He and his wife and daughter and grandchild, his daughter's husband, and a grandson and brother-in-law have made expeditions to the Kenai for sockeye most of the last six years. There are two heads of households involved in the group, so that accounts for fifty fish alone. Then there are the kids. Ten more fish for each. A couple of years ago Hancock, fifty-nine, had the best single red fishing day of his life.

"We were pulling them in as fast as we could," Hancock said. "We caught twenty-five in a half hour. One time my brother-in-law made a mountain out of fish heads and seagull feathers on the beach."

The water can be rough at times, too. Hancock's sixteen-year-old granddaughter once went out a bit too far and water swamped her waders.

"My brother-in-law picked her up and turned her upside down to let the water run out," Hancock said. "I'm surprised a big salmon didn't fall out. It should have been on *America's Funniest Home Videos*."

Hancock said he loves the gentler summer weather in Alaska—no humidity, frequent sunshine, and comfortable temperatures. He no longer fishes with rod and reel because of all the time it takes to catch a king salmon. "I got burned out on it," he said.

Living in Alaska for years before he went subsistence fishing earlier this decade, Hancock said he enjoyed the heck out of his first time. It was a sunny day, with temperatures in the seventies, about as nice as it ever gets in Southcentral Alaska. "I was so excited, the first fish I got I fell in the water," Hancock said. "It was just the excitement of catching one, the exhilaration of catching one."

Hancock was working in his south Anchorage shop the day he reminisced about his reds journey, but was planning another assault a couple of days later and was monitoring the Fish and Game daily sockeye count at the sonar measuring point. Some 120,000 fish had entered the river the day before. He seemed to be timing the trip just right.

After Hancock's scheduled fishing trip, I touched base with him and discovered that the 2012 reds adventure for his family had not panned out as hoped. "It was a disaster," he said, starting with the fact that "there were a million people there" and it was difficult to eke out fishing space. That turned out to be only a minor impediment.

Hancock had just begun his Kenai Walk. Ten minutes after he started fishing he was alerted that his vehicle, which he had loaned to a friend, had broken down. He had to leave the fishing grounds, find his truck, and get it to a repair shop. He got the vehicle back to Anchorage and suffered the indignity of a $900 bill for the breakdown.

The rest of the family stayed on the Kenai to maintain the honor of the group. Only the fishing turned flat. "They stayed down there a few more days," Hancock said, "and they caught two fish a day. It's the worst dipnetting we've ever had. I guess there are good times and bad times."

DON'T BREAK THE RULES

On the morning of my next mid-July fishing trip I picked up the *Anchorage Daily News* and saw a headline that grabbed me: "Former Guide Gets 60 Days." Well, a fishing guide has to be a bad boy to find himself in the crosshairs of law enforcement officers.

This one was. The guide, who was from Cooper Landing, earned himself a sixty-day sentence, three years probation, and was ordered to pay $17,229.55 in restitution. He pled guilty to stealing from nearly seventy fishing clients.

Whoa! He didn't steal their fish, but the operator of Wise Guide Outfitters acted more like Wise Guy Outfitters by bilking clients of their deposits. The guide, who actually had relocated to Utah, was charged with selling Alaska fishing vacations on eBay, starting in 2005.

Demonstrating great enthusiasm, anglers signed up for fishing trips, but the guide flaked out on delivering them. In his courtroom testimony the man said he got overbooked, took on more trips than he could handle, and couldn't deliver the goods paid for.

"I screwed up," the repentant guide said. "I wasn't mentally stable and have since started taking medication."

Mr. Guide said he was now gainfully employed in Utah and so could afford to pay $500 a month in restitution after he got out of jail. However, the judge ruled that he couldn't leave the state until he paid off at least 50 percent of that bill. I wondered how that dilemma would be resolved. In addition, there was an aside that indicated left-at-the-altar clients were not precluded from pursuing civil cases against the guide.

Moral of the story: It's one thing to go fishless by being skunked after putting in your time on the river, but it's quite another to go fishless because you were ripped off in advance.

MY NEW FRIEND FLY BOB

When I met Bob Overman at the Russian River in June and he told me that he guided fishermen for reds, I perked up. No ferry? No combat fishing? Sounded as if it was worth trying, so we agreed to hook up in July for the second run of reds and I assumed that since every other Kenai River guide I'd ever met used a boat we would be going out in a boat.

I kept right on assuming that until I rendezvoused with Bob and his dog Barney and learned that we were going in on foot.

"I'm a walking guide," Overman said.

Oh.

Despite his nickname of "Fly Bob," I also checked to make sure we weren't fly fishing. Fly fishing and I do not get along well. I am definitely somewhat of a menace trying to cast with a fly rod.

"We're using a fly rod, but we're not fly fishing," Overman said.

The equipment, the rods, and the place were all new to me. Our approach to the river off the highway was in Sterling, not Soldotna, and we were headed for the Naptown Rapids area and Bob had a spot picked out where we could fish from the bank. It was not a secret spot since other regulars congregated there, but it was not a very large area, so only about a dozen fishermen at once could be accommodated.

This was also not a place where you could just park your car and trot across the parking lot twenty yards and be on the water. Nothing was that easy. It was about a quarter-mile hike on a narrow, muddy trail to a bluff. There was a steep staircase for some of the downward plunge, but much of the way required scrambling down the steep hill, grabbing onto ropes placed there so we didn't slip. Klutzes need not apply.

Bob Overman, known as Fly Bob, is a walking guide for the Kenai River, leading those who don't know the area to selected spots to fish for red salmon. Overman survived a life-threatening fall through the ice into the river last winter and had to be rescued.

Slightly built, with a white beard, Overman, who is a cook by profession, and is a winter property caretaker in Cooper Landing, was fifty-seven, but could have been anything within ten years of that number in either direction. He accidentally became a walking guide about six years earlier when someone asked him for help targeting sockeyes. His modus operandi is that any excuse to go fishing will do at any time of the year.

Over the winter he ties thousands of flies for amusement, to stay busy, and to stock up for spring and summer. He has developed his own approach and manner for chasing the three reds permitted on a daily basis, but he never forgets where he is, either. When the fish are running, not only do the seagulls line up for eats, but the black and brown bears that roam the Kenai Peninsula in abundance know the river is the easiest place to find food. Bears gorge on salmon and if you happen to choose a bear's favorite fishing spot to set up, it is a no-brainer to realize just who is going to win that territorial rights argument. When Overman goes fishing on days like this one where a healthy walk is required in and out of the fishing spot on a narrow path like the one we used, he comes prepared.

Tucked in the front of his chest waders, Overman carried a handgun that was as imposing as any bear claw. This was no derringer. Think *Dirty Harry*. Yes, Overman answered to my query about bears in the neighborhood. Yes there are.

"They have followed us all the way down and made us move," he said.

I had been a regular at the river since April and I had yet to see a bear in the flesh on the Kenai. Of course I knew they were there, but at most I hoped to see bears prowling in the distance this summer. So far they were nonexistent to me. But not to others. Victor Senethep, twenty, of Anchorage, was fishing on the Kenai River as often as he could make the trip all summer, and although he proclaimed it "a great year for reds," it sounded as if he had seen as many bears as fish, or at least as many bears as I had seen eagles.

There was the black bear seventy-five yards away on the shore of the Russian River. "We stopped fishing right away," Senethep said. "We packed our stuff right away and went. It felt like it was too interested."

Another time he saw a grizzly sow with two cubs. They were within fifty yards. A mama bear with her babies is about the most dangerous beast in the wild in Alaska. "That was close," Senethep said. "A couple of days later I saw them again. They were eating all of the carcasses. I would throw mine to them."

For a few minutes, Senethep devoted his entire attention to the bears, putting down his fishing rod. He pulled out his cell phone and focused the camera on them as they roamed the opposite shore of the swiftly flowing river. That seemed like a safe distance. He recorded the bears for a few minutes and then the bears began crossing the river. Show's over. "We ran," he said.

Bears make for dangerous fishing companions along the Kenai River and anglers are wise to take heed of warnings that they could pop up at any time.

Throwing fish guts to bears is a deal with the devil and can be risky, so it made sense to be ready to run then, too. Bears can move at lightning speed when they want to, covering fifty yards in seconds. It is always prudent to yield a spot to a bear and give up the fish if they are too inquisitive.

Senethep lamented that he did not catch a king salmon that spring, but did say he had already hauled in a couple of silvers. The funny thing is, as much as he loves fishing, he doesn't like to eat fish and pretty much gives away his entire catch. "I'd rather eat burgers or chicken," Senethep said.

The area staked out to fish by Overman didn't leave much running room if a bear wandered our way. We stood on the edge of the water, or in it, and if we wanted to sit down for a breather at any point we could climb a couple of feet up the steep bluff and rest on a rock.

"I love it here," Overman said. "I catch a lot of fish here. When the pinks start running you're into a fish every cast."

It was one of those days when the Kenai River was a brilliant turquoise color and it was a good enough day to fish that anglers stood about eight feet apart in this little corner of the shore, carefully trying to stay clear of one another, but also maneuvering for enough space to cast and catch their three-red limit. "If I can get this spot, this spot, or this spot, I can guarantee I'm gonna catch fish," Overman said.

At the moment, all three spots were occupied, so we waited our turn, either for the fishermen to catch their limits or for them to get bored and leave.

Overman launched into his tutorial for my benefit. "Sometimes the tip of the rod will just bend a little bit," he said of the feel of a bite on his gear. "It might be just a peck, peck, and all of a sudden the water will just explode. Other times the hit is like a rocket. Every fish is a little bit different. I love the ones that explode on you."

Every fisherman loves to see a fish surface heartily hooked, jumping out of the water, splashing. If the fish is truly hooked in the jaw the fight is a good one and there is no danger it will toss the hook. Those are the ones you see on videos on TV outdoors shows. If the hook is not set, the fight may be fleeting and the fish will escape. They never show those.

My biggest problem was adapting to the fly fishing-like conditions. Fishing for kings involves sitting in a boat with the line dangling over the side. Likewise in silver fishing. Dipnetting involves the use of a wide-mouthed net. Fishing for reds from shore with Overman's equipment meant casting a line into the air with a certain motion that he called "'the Kenai flip.' You won't do that anywhere else."

Depending on where I was fishing, I have often cast sidearm because I found it more effective and less threatening to life around me. That was out of the question here. Had to be overhand, my weakness, and I also had to twist my wrist on the delivery, something difficult for me since I had long ago broken my right wrist. Suddenly, I was in one of those deals were I hoped to avoid humiliation. I didn't want to hit anyone fishing near me. I didn't want to hurt anyone. I didn't want to have to apologize to anyone every five minutes. Those were all higher priorities than catching a sockeye, although, damn it, I wanted to do that, too.

The Kenai flip, here I come. But were the fish coming? Glancing around me at the catches of others who had been hovering on the bank for some time, my evaluation was that the fishing was so-so. Fish were out there, but not in the masses that often make men marvel.

"I've had them hit me in the boot," Overman said of the reds rushing past as he stood a foot deep in the river. "They've been so thick you could walk across the river on them."

I took that as a metaphor, not a literal statement. The Kenai flip did not come naturally to me. Rather than a smooth follow-through I broke my wrist. That meant that the cast was erratic. I was slow on the uptake to the technique.

"Right here is the best bait fishing on the Kenai as far as walking in," Overman said.

He launched into a scientific analysis of the way the sockeyes swam and adapted to the underwater curve of the river and a few more comments that led to the conclusion "They're gonna funnel right by you."

One of our fishing neighbors was Terry Nix, a regular in this spot, but also someone who branches out to the Russian River and the Anchor River on the way to Homer for coho and Chinook salmon. When the red fishing is really hot, Nix said, it's possible to see five or six of them on hooks at once.

"To me there's nothing like hitting a big red for toughness the way they fight," he said. "I lost a ten or twelve pounder. It wiggled off right between my legs."

"Fly Bob" Overman had some action going, but it didn't last long.

"Was that a fish?" Nix asked of the escapee.

Overman had a disgusted look on his face. "I'd call it a Dolly," he said. Fly Bob studied my casting form critically, then said, "I think you've got it. It's not something you're going to use on any other river."

The pace of reds grabbing hooks increased. "Here they come," Nix said.

Sometimes when a fish is lured in, it plays with bait, or the hook, and just nibbles, determining whether what's being offered is something it wants to eat. Other times the slam is so hard the rod bends in half and there is no wondering about the hit. Fly Bob had one of those.

"That's a fish," he said.

About six of us stood in a row on a chunk of rocky shore trying not to collide, but trying to coax those reds out of the water. To our right where the shore bent out of view, a handful of others fished. Suddenly, fish began grabbing their lines. The action was headed our way. But for some reason the fish did not attack our lines with the same ferocity. The other group picked them off steadily, but we were only getting one here and one there. Fly Bob started reeling in a fish, but came up empty-handed. "I lost it all," he said sadly. "Hook, line, sinker. A rock cleaned my clock."

A few raindrops fell and I was not excited about the prospect of the limited ground around us turning all muddy. Overman had been fishing a day earlier when everybody got soaked. "I was so wet yesterday I looked like a drowned puppy," he said.

Weather was not something that would interfere with either Fly Bob or Nix going out fishing for a day. It might be an inconvenience, but not something significant enough to keep them home.

"You're in the presence of two fishing maniacs," Nix said. "Fishaholics," Fly Bob said. "When I tell my wife I'm going fishing, she knows I'm going fishing," Nix added.

Nix, who had been fishing since the middle of the night, decided to knock off before we did, with only two fish, not his three-fish limit. He lost one up close, but the pace of fish being caught was slowing and he didn't know how much longer it might take to nab that third one. "I'm satisfied," Nix said. "It's a damn shame that I lost the one on the bank. I could have been done hours ago."

Some anglers went home, others slid into their spots. There were fish around, but it was not one of those days where they were going to swim into your feet. The sun came out and then rain clouds returned. Back and forth. The river provided backup noise without being roaring loud.

A fish flew out of the water, eliciting oohs and ahs from those that saw it leap. Reds are sometimes difficult to wrangle once hooked. They get angry, try to spit the hook, and make a run for it. For fishermen the trump card is the net if they can get the fish close enough for a swipe.

After a while of Kenai flipping my arm got tired, the fingers on my right hand got stiff, and my back ached. Overman rolled along and hooked a red that he instantly recognized as being a big one. He didn't even try to net it. Instead, he dragged it all of the way in and up on shore. Holy moley, it did look big, at least twelve pounds. "That is a hog," Overman said. Another angler nearby gazed at the fish and said, "Oh, man, that's a football."

Even Barney, a shepherd, husky mix, who had been rather casual about the day's proceedings until then, seemed intrigued by the fish flopping on the ground. A well-behaved, friendly dog, I couldn't help but wonder if I yelled, "Go fetch!" if he wouldn't have dashed into the water and caught me a fish.

While I rested and Nix packed up, he asked if Fly Bob had told me the story of how he almost drowned in the river. That was a new topic for me and I gradually got filled in by Bob about what happened to make the Kenai turn ugly on him.

Overman doesn't actually believe there is such thing as a fishing season. If there is water showing in the Kenai River that means it's a good time to fish. Even if the surrounding area is snowbound, or the temperature is ten degrees. In late February there was some open water on the Kenai at the bridge in Cooper Landing and Overman went fly fishing.

Actually, Overman doesn't have any trouble remember the date or the time. It was February 25, and it was just after 9 A.M. when he was walking on the ice on the river. He came with a friend but they had separated a good distance to fish. The ice gave way with no warning and Overman plummeted into the freezing water. The river is pretty shallow in most parts and it is even shallower in most places in winter.

"I stepped on thin ice and went through and I thought I would only fall a couple of inches," he said. However, although he was just ten feet from shore, Overman happened to be walking right above a hole that he later guessed was about eighteen feet deep. Shocked, he fought back to the surface, but could not lift himself onto the solid ice. He began yelling for help, but no one else was fishing close by and he believed if his friend heard him initially he mistook his cries of alarm for yells of joy in catching a big fish.

Overman's situation quickly became dire. It doesn't take more than a few minutes to drain someone's energy in cold water. He was able to cling to the edge of the ice and finally make himself heard. Alerted, help rushed to the river where a member of Cooper Land Volunteer Fire & Rescue and an Alaska Wildlife Trooper jump-started a rescue plan. They had to employ caution and couldn't get too close to Overman, lest they collapse more of the ice and also fall into the water. At first Overman was thrown a rope, but said it was too short and he didn't have the strength to pull himself over the lip of the ice.

Next, a parachute cord was tied to a backpack and heaved in Overman's direction, but that didn't work. Another member of the Cooper Landing rescue team arrived on the scene with a stronger rope that he shaped into a lasso. He heaved it to Overman, who wrapped it around his arm, and as he held tight the men yanked him free of the water and to safety.

"It was pretty scary," said Overman, who remembered that much.

Some onsite medical treatment began because Overman was so cold. His wet waders and clothing were sliced off his body.

"They were getting ready to start CPR on me," he recalled. He said he mumbled, "I'm good. I'm good to go." Go he did.

Overman said he had never flown in his life, but was airlifted in a helicopter to the hospital.

"My first flight ever and I did it naked," he said.

While the experience was life threatening and frightening, not even eighteen minutes floating in potentially deadly water meant that Fly Bob will forego engaging in winter fishing on the Kenai River.

"Now I know where that hole is," he said.

We called it a day after four hours of fishing and retraced our steps over that path. No bears were seen. Got a few fish on the day, but the cool air helped us build an appetite. Not two minutes from the turnoff road from the river to the main highway, what had been a wildlife-free day ended. No, bears weren't darting across the street, but a mother moose and two young ones ran flat out across the highway dodging cars that weren't paying attention.

While Fly Bob and I both spotted the erratically jogging moose, a driver on our right didn't see them and while he was passing he nearly clipped one of the small moose.

"I think momma would have charged that car if he picked off one of the babies," Bob said.

It was a close call, but carnage was avoided.

JUST A FRIENDLY LITTLE COMPETITION

When the World Wrestling Federation facsimile belt was held high and Kevin Day danced around with it, I knew I had stepped into the middle of some serious business.

I was the odd man out, the accidental tourist, fishing with Mike Fenton on this mid-July day, along with a slew of other boats Fenton Brothers sent out onto the Kenai River to catch king salmon. Everyone else was part of a team, either UPS pilots of Alaska or FedEx pilots of Alaska.

Anchorage is a major freight hub for the two businesses that fly around the world with cargo. Day, who is originally from Maine, and Tim Brown, who works for UPS, grew up together in Maine and years later found they were coincidentally both stationed in Anchorage for the competing freight companies. They began having fishing showdowns with one another and have expanded the annual fish-off to include several coworkers. Never before has there been such a special prize at stake as a fake heavyweight wrestling championship belt.

Besides, pride of company was at issue in the fishing showdown. It was a day of company bonding through silliness, for the most part, I gathered, when I heard one group shout, "Tastes great!" and the other group shout, "Less filling!" The humorous beer ads those opinions derived from had come and gone, but the slogan lived on.

The teams were divided up between various boats. Although I had no particular allegiance to one company or the other, based on seat availability I was assigned a spot with Cindy Freier, Scott Nelson, and Mike Teo from UPS to fish with Mike Fenton, but nothing I caught would count toward the king poundage or fish numbers total. There was no fudging it when the coveted prize plastic title belt was on the line.

We all climbed into the boat and Fenton turned to one client and asked, "You want to go by Bob, or Robert?" Actually, he wanted to go by Scott because that was his name. I asked Fenton if he wanted to go by Mike or Murray. He decided to stick with his own identity and not borrow his brother's.

Scott had a pressing question. He wanted to know how he could tell when a king salmon took his line. "It's gonna hit like a ton of bricks," Fenton said.

Soon enough, Scott did have a bite and reeled in a fish after a five-minute fight. "One for UPS," Cindy cheered. "Nice going, Scotty!" a UPS coworker from another boat yelled over.

Scott was not experienced in Kenai River king salmon fishing, but he had been king fishing on Lake Michigan. Many Alaska fishermen don't even know that you can catch salmon on Lake Michigan, right offshore of the mammoth

Mike Fenton, one of two siblings running Fenton Brothers guide service, is about to clean a fish at the end a Kenai River trip.

city of Chicago. Lake Michigan, one of the Great Lakes, and the fifth largest lake in the world, has been stocked with salmon for decades.

The salmon fishery has been thriving on Lake Michigan for ages. You can catch Chinook salmon and coho salmon, but the style and limits are totally different from those fishing on the Kenai. Much larger, sturdier boats are needed on the lake because of the potential for violent wave action unlike the benign Kenai. The Great Lakes are known as the United States' third ocean, and anyone who has heard the Gordon Lightfoot song "The Wreck of the Edmund Fitzgerald," about how Lake Superior devoured that freighter in a storm in November of 1975, should understand the power in those waters. Fishing might entail going offshore for miles, too. A big king on Lake Michigan is seventeen pounds, nothing like the sixty-pound-plus models offered on the Kenai, and sometimes the kings and silvers might mix in the catch. The daily limit is five, which makes for a fun day of fishing, but from personal experience I can say that when you grill them or otherwise prepare them for dinner, they just can't measure up to the taste of Kenai River wild salmon.

"The biggest king I ever caught on Lake Michigan was twenty pounds," Scott said. "Here it's not like a lake trout. You can feel the weight. It was like bringing up a wet boot."

Scott is from Deerfield, Illinois, so came by his Great Lakes fishing naturally. Fenton estimated this Kenai king Scott caught as thirty-eight inches long and such a length indicated it was probably around thirty-eight pounds. The fish not only rolled above the surface once but also came in pretty easily. "Not often do they come out of the water like that," Fenton said. "It's a crowd pleaser."

As we motored to different spots seeking more kings, we saw numerous people red fishing. The reds were in and the crowds had massed. The fact that our boat had a king was noteworthy given how the season had gone.

Clucking with a sigh, Fenton said this might be a day of reckoning with kings on the Kenai after so many years of good runs. "We knew this day was coming," Fenton said with a fisherman's pessimism. "It's like the perfect storm."

To Fenton the perfect storm was essentially the laundry list of reasons other people had enunciated searching out explanations for the missing fish. All of the ocean possibilities were mentioned, commercial fishermen, unusually high water in the river. All could be culprits, Fenton said.

Whatever was afflicting the species and scaring them away from our lines, Scott didn't seem to have much trouble communicating with the fish. He added a rainbow trout to his score.

This was a bunch in a party mood and good fishing will help the mood of any party on the water. The challenge to a guide to entertain for a day that was going to run about eight hours was how to keep anglers happy and interested when the fish didn't cooperate. After twenty-five years on the Kenai, though, Mike Fenton had a storehouse of stories to tell.

"Did you know I set a world record on the Kenai?" he said. Who can resist an opening like that? On July 31, 1986, Fenton was fishing for sockeyes from shore on the Middle River when he hooked a king salmon. A fish had rolled in front of him and he cast with the belief he was chasing a red. It was unusual enough for Fenton to catch a king in that area, but he was only using twelve-pound test line. That is so flimsy the king should have been able to snap it off with a shrug of its head.

It took a moment for Fenton to realize what he'd hooked and he had to think fast how to handle it. If he was not super careful the fish would break his line. He had to nurse it and let the fish lead him, so he jumped into a nearby boat, kept the hook in and the fish on, but did only the most delicate of reeling until the fish was too weary to go on. Then Fenton ever-so-gently reeled it to the boat and hauled it in.

The king weighed sixty-seven and one-quarter pounds, a remarkable catch on twelve-pound test, something more suitable to use in catching a small catfish or something of that ilk. The International Game Fish Association in Florida certified Fenton's record. Some fishermen read the record book and try to break existing records for catching certain-sized fish on light tackle. That was not Fenton's objective that day. He was as surprised as the fish. When an onlooker marveled at how big the Chinook was on the skinny line, the record book was consulted.

"It wasn't that I was targeting the record," Fenton said.

Fenton paused, gave a deadpan look to our crowd, and said, "I've got 'World Record Holder' tattooed on my chest."

Yuk, yuk, yuk, as the Three Stooges would say. Fenton was making a joke. Good story, no tattoo.

If you guide for a quarter of a century, some weird things are bound to happen, and Fenton has had his share. About ten years ago he had a marriage proposal in his boat. The prospective groom tied a $10,000 ring on the end of his line and then had his potential bride reel it in. It was a bold gesture, but the guy was apparently premature in his enthusiasm.

When the ring came up from the deep he asked the gal to marry him. And the response? "It was kind of a little hesitation thing," Fenton said. But she said yes and they broke out the champagne.

Soul mates as they seemed, each of them caught a big king salmon that day. The guy caught a sixty-pound female and his date caught a sixty-pound male. Nice symmetry, huh? Champagne, a fancy ring, big fish, it sounded like a grand day all around. There was only one problem. "They ended up never getting married," Fenton said.

That event did not quite live up to its potential, but about seven years ago Fenton did have a marriage take place on his boat. It should be no surprise to hear that the wedding—exactly at noon—occurred at Honeymoon Cove, one of the Kenai's hot fishing spots.

"They'd fished with us for a few years before that," Fenton said. "They wanted me to marry them."

Fenton's raconteuring was interrupted by a fish on. Cindy had her king. The fish hit and stayed bit. It wasn't getting off. Cindy reeled the fish to the boat, Fenton looked it over, and released it. "You had that baby hooked," he said. He figured the length at twenty-eight inches.

"I think I get a huge high five for that," Cindy said and teammate Mike Teo obliged her.

We hunkered down with hoods over our heads and put hands in pockets as Fenton took us on a long ride after that to settle into another allegedly good fishing spot. Even with sunshine once we moved and created some wind we got cold. When the boat cruised to a stop, Teo said, "Now that we're frozen . . ."

The fish took another hiatus and Fenton regaled us with some more tales from the Guide's Greatest Hits album. Once upon a time he was guiding a family and the woman was wearing a blue rain bonnet. Whoosh, it blew off in the wind and headed downriver near Sunken Island. It blew too far away to grab and soon after it sank beneath the surface. Wave good-bye to the rain bonnet, ma'am.

"Sometimes strange things happen," Fenton said, setting up the next chapter in this story. "We were fishing way downriver and the woman's rod goes down."

Fish on! Lots of excitement in the boat. She reels and reels and at last the fish comes to the side of the boat. Only it isn't a fish at all. Eleven miles downriver, the woman caught her own rain bonnet.

"Is that bizarre or what?" Fenton said.

Fenton even had a story that originated with brother Murray, a secondhand tale. Not every single client is a nominee for Miss Congeniality or Mr. Sunnyside Up. One day, Murray had a grumpy fellow in his boat. He kept the air pungent with a cigar and was critical because they weren't catching fish.

"The guy's kind of a jerk," Mike Fenton said. "Murray's working his butt off to get him a fish and on the very last pass of the day the guy finally gets a bite." Murray warned the man to be careful and set the hook properly. He started reeling and then he leaned forward and the lit end of the cigar alighted on the line, cutting the line with the cigar. Good-bye, fish. "Couldn't have happened to a nicer guy," Mike Fenton said.

About ten years ago, Mike Fenton had two honeymoon couples in his boat and they were gabbing away. He asked where they were from and one of the women said she was from Snohomish, Washington. Fenton thought that was pretty neat-o because he was also from Snohomish. He had been looking this babe over all day and thought she looked kind of familiar. But when she said Snohomish and he said Snohomish, it hit them. This lady was exactly who he thought it was. And it dawned on her at the same time, too. Some twenty or twenty-five years earlier they had once had a summer romance. Well, sort of.

"I think I got to third base," Fenton said.

That was not the time to mention old acquaintances, however, although they did have a few minutes to chat after the trip. That was probably one of the stranger client encounters Fenton ever had.

Sometimes a fishing story can be heartwarming, not humorous. About fifteen years ago Fenton was guiding three middle-aged guys and their father. They were in their forties, but the old man really was old, and he was suffering from cancer. This was a last special trip for the men in the family to share.

One by one the sons each caught a good-sized king salmon. Pop had hooked a couple of fish, but hadn't hung on to any of them. They got away.

Fishing, then, as now, ended at 6 P.M. and Fenton glanced at his watch. It was past 5:30 P.M. "I've got to get this guy a fish," he thought.

The clock touched 6 P.M. and Fenton said, "We gave it a hell of a shot, buddy." The second the words were out of his mouth the father's rod bent in half. "I go, 'Oh, my god, we've got a fish on.'" Once the fish was hooked it was legal to keep after it and complete the catch, even though it was then past the six o'clock cutoff. The man was in a fairly weakened state, so there was no guarantee he was going to be able to haul in the king on his own, but he gave it all the muscle he had. It was a real tug of war between him and the fish.

"The boys are with him cheering him on," Fenton said. "It took us an hour to get that fish in. It was a sixty-five pounder. There we were, five grown men and we were just crying like babies. You know he passed away not even a month later." But a photograph endures of the event, the three sons and their dad and one big, honking fish on the last great trip of a lifetime.

Unfortunately for us, our boat was not going to limit out with a king for everyone. The bite was slow, so that was discouraging, but Fenton had a grand repertoire of stories in his memory bank.

This fellow in his twenties had fished with Fenton once before and four years ago booked another trip. This time he was coming from the Lower 48 with a friend of his and his friend's father. They were traveling north to fish for silver salmon and rainbow trout. But before they made the trek they called back to ask Fenton what type of payment he accepted. He said, "credit card, check, or green stuff." He thought the message was clear enough.

Well, when it came time to settle up accounts, one of the guys leaned into Fenton and stuffed something in his pocket. He didn't know what it was. Fenton looked at what the man stuck in his pocket and was startled to see a small bag. "It was marijuana, not that I would know," said Fenton batting his eyelashes innocently. Expecting money, Fenton said, "I thought he gave me the wrong bag or something."

Fenton leaned in and said to the guy, "You gave me the wrong bag," and handed it back to him. The man stuffed it back in Fenton's pocket and said, "Green stuff." I said, "Oh, my god." Fenton informed the gentleman that his definition of green stuff was cash. "He got this white look on his face. He's totally embarrassed."

Not only has the guy never come back to fish with Fenton on the Kenai again, but when Fenton telephoned him to see if he wanted a return trip—after all he was already a repeat customer—he didn't return the phone calls.

Whether it was his personality, guide reputation, or something else, over the years during the Kenai Classic Fenton became the regular guide for Senator Ted Stevens. Somehow they hit it off and were together on the river for several years. Given Stevens's importance to the founding and continuation of the Classic the organizers always wanted to make sure he was happy. If Fenton made Stevens happy, then everyone was happy.

During one Classic, however, Fenton had a close call with his precious cargo. Stevens hooked a fish. He was standing at the back end of the boat trying to wrestle it in. Sometimes a big king will pull hard when the fisherman least expects it and that might have been what happened this day. Fenton intently watched the fight and to his horror he sensed that Stevens had lost his balance and was in danger of a plunge into the forty-five-degree water.

Fenton lunged across the boat, grabbed the senator by his coat, and pulled him back from the edge. "He almost fell in," Fenton said.

That was a type of publicity Fenton didn't need. He imagined what the newspaper headlines would have been like if US Senator Ted Stevens went overboard. "They probably would have read, 'Dumbshit Guide Pushes Senator Stevens in Water,'" Fenton said.

Time ran out on the UPS-FedEx showdown. It was a full day on the river and not many kings were caught, but scrupulous count was made of those that were and their weights. This is when the championship belt came out, as well as information about its origins. Kevin Day of Anchorage FedEx had gone on a shopping expedition to the Fred Meyer store and found this fabulous belt for $20.

"The first year I won," Day said. "Last year we kind of had a tie." Brown chimed in: "My fish was longer."

It really was a small-world thing that these men who fly all around the world are from the same state thousands of miles away and both ended up in Alaska. "He used to date my sister," Day said.

This was the third year of the fish-off and this year both men brought backup. It was pretty clear when everyone disembarked from boats at the dock that UPS was not going to have possession of the belt very long. The

Tim Brown, a UPS pilot based in Anchorage, shows off the fake World Wrestling Federation belt that was at stake during a fish-off against the FedEx pilots of Anchorage.

big fish winner of the day was Matt Evans of FedEx, who caught a fifty-inch king salmon.

"It was a thirty-minute fight," Evans said. "It was awesome. It was taking 150 feet of line and then it jumped out of the water three times. It was a fun fight." And then Evans pinned the fish, or rather reeled it up to the boat.

Not surrendering easily, Day tried to claim a prize for the smallest fish of the day. He caught a four-inch Dolly Varden. "I win the booby prize for smallest fish," he said.

In the end the belt changed hands and UPS vowed, Wait till next year.

STILL MISSING KINGS

As the summer went on more king salmon did appear in the Kenai River, but never in the numbers that Fish and Game wanted to see in order to liberalize fishing regulations. Everyone had a theory as to where the fish had all gone, but the universal sentiment was sadness over something being lost that we thought would be a reliable fixture forever.

In the early 2000s, before my wife Debra was my wife Debra and just my friend Debra I took her on her first fishing trip to the Kenai River. We fished the Upper River out of a raft with Gary Galbraith and we fished the Lower River with Joe Hanes, one of the long-term veterans of the area.

I don't know whether it was my bad luck rubbing off or some other voodoo at work, but no king salmon were caught on this journey. Debra cynically joked that the entire Kenai River fishing legend was a hoax. There was no such thing as king salmon in the river. Years later, during this fish famine, she reminded me of her early comments and used the current-day example to claim she had been right all along. I wish I could have thought of a clever retort, but there wasn't much to say about the absence of kings that was funny.

It should be noted that Debra did catch a fish on the Kenai with Galbraith presiding. Although professing to not knowing what she was doing the entire time she reeled it in, Deb caught a twenty-two-inch rainbow trout as several of us cheered her on.

"I did everything wrong," she said.

"You got the fish," Galbraith said. "It's better to be lucky than good."

Checking some of my older scribblings I realized that during the trip with Hanes it was discovered that one angler had a bunch of bananas in his cooler for refreshment. This was quite alarming and if lore could be believed was the cause of our trip being doomed. With an aplomb rarely seen in a guide when the topic turns to bananas, Hanes said he wasn't bothered a bit by their presence. Surprised me. However, he did add that if the fishing wasn't going well the first thing being ditched overboard was going to be the bananas. Eat fast, buddy, I thought of the perpetrator.

During that Kenai fishing trip with Debra, Hanes reflected in a way about king salmon and the river that seemed particularly apropos in 2012 in light of the Chinook shortage we were confronted by. "It's like the last refuge of where you hear the largest salmon in the world swim," Hanes said of the Kenai River. "It's the lure of the value of that and the challenge of preserving it. We're trying to do something here that's never been done in the history of mankind. We're trying to save a race of salmon."

Hanes's thoughts were definitely something to chew on a good piece of a decade later.

Les Palmer is a longtime Alaska outdoors writer who pens a column for the *Peninsula Clarion*, the Kenai Peninsula's daily newspaper, and by July, he, like everyone else around, was perplexed and concerned about what happened to the salmon.

"Since the early 1970s, when I first started fishing Kenai Peninsula waters, this is the first year I haven't fished for king salmon in a stream," Palmer wrote in a mid-July piece. "It's also the first time I haven't cooked a first-king-of-the-year to celebrate the occasion. I'm not alone. The fish that put Soldotna on the map has let everyone down."

Just another glimpse of what others were thinking about the situation.

In mid-July, about fifty fishermen held a demonstration at the Alaska Fish and Game office in Soldotna, calling their cause a "King Salmon Preservation Rally." Since it was not in Fish and Game's power to magically make kings appear, what the fishermen tried to do was make a statement that if there was a shortage of kings in the river and they couldn't fish for them, then commercial set-netters shouldn't be allowed to fish for them either. After all, a king salmon was a king salmon was a king salmon, regardless of who caught it and ate it.

Around that time the *Anchorage Daily News* ran an intriguing story about a topic that might have had repercussions on salmon. Meteorologists announced it was the coldest July on record in Anchorage. It is never what the average American would consider toasty warm in Anchorage. In the seventeen years I lived in the state the highest temperature I encountered in Anchorage was one eighty-two-degree day. A gorgeous summer day is in the low seventies. More typical are days in the sixties.

But Anchorage was missing both sunshine and warmth. The average temperature in July was running at under fifty-three degrees. Plus, buckets of rain were falling. The irony of seeing that story was that flying through Chicago on my way to Anchorage I read a story in the *Chicago Tribune* saying it was the hottest July on record in the Lower 48.

No one was doing the study for the Kenai-Soldotna area, but the weather is not usually dramatically different from Anchorage and residents certainly recognized that July was chillier than the norm. And so was the water temperature. Over at Harry Gaines Kenai River Fishing, Reuben Hanke said the river temperature was about three degrees colder than it should have been. Whether that reflected the unusually cool air, or the snowmelt from the mountains from the record snowfall of the winter, or both, no one could say. How that all affected the salmon no one could say either. Blaming mysterious doings in the ocean ranked higher on the likely problem list.

August

KENAI RIVER JUNIOR CLASSIC

Kids poured onto the land behind the Harry Gaines fish camp at what seemed to be the same rate as reds pouring into the Kenai River at the height of the run. Big yellow school buses rolled up and disgorged boys and girls between ten and sixteen years old, ready to be introduced to the joys of fishing for salmon.

About 110 kids from Joint Base Elmendorf-Richardson in Anchorage and some Girl Scouts were brought in for the sixth annual event that is the child of the original Kenai Classic. Elmendorf Air Force Base and Fort Richardson go back to World War II, but only recently merged. Each year a different group of kids are invited to participate in the Kids Classic as this event is sometimes called. Organizers felt the children of active duty service personnel who might be in Afghanistan probably could use some relaxation.

The hosting Kenai River Sportfishing Association also thought it was a pretty good idea to introduce kids to the pleasures of the Kenai River at a young age. Maybe as they grew up they would become rabid fishermen. Maybe after they grew up they would attain positions of prominence in the world and become influential politicians or corporate figures with the power to pass legislation or public policy that would help preserve the river. Or they maybe they would just have a heck of a good time.

There is a fellow in Chicago who works for the city's recreational department and in the summer oversees a program that introduces thousands of kids to fishing. They use the city's stocked lagoons for instruction and year after year it's a parade of youths to the waters. Program director Bob Long's theory is a simple one: If you teach a child to fish he will always come back to it at some point in his life. He may get distracted by girls for a while. Families might be raised. But eventually, he will return to fishing.

Bob Penney liked that theory. It sounded right to him, though he was focused more on immediate dividends than futuristic ones.

"You show me a kid who likes to fish and do things in the outdoors and he's not doing drugs," Penney said. "They learn respect for the river and for the fish. I was seven or eight years old when my dad took me fishing. I caught my first king salmon when I was fourteen. It weighed seventeen pounds and I thought it was the greatest thing. I got hooked at the same time as the fish."

Penney turned out to watch the goings-on for a while although he was not going out on the river this day. He was a behind-the-scenes guy. A little bit more out front was US Senator Lisa Murkowski. Murkowski, as one of the national representatives for the Kenai River, in a way is a stand-in for the late Senator Ted Stevens. She was involved in the July Classic and was back in the neighborhood for this event. You can bet Penney has spent hours keeping her up-to-date on the issues, the conservation status, and the problems revolving around the Kenai River, just as he bent Senator Mark Begich's ear the time he essentially kidnapped him and drove the senator around and around Kenai after picking him up at the airport. When it comes to the Kenai River, Penney is never going to be shy. Anyone who could be an ally will be enlisted in the Kenai cause.

While the kids were massing, being organized, and outfitted with life jackets, I wandered next door for the first time in years. The next-door-neighbor summer home is owned by the family of one of Harry Gaines's best friends. Dean Yeasel and his wife, Phyllis, lived out of state, but spent summers right here overlooking the Kenai River and I saw them frequently. During the sad summer after Harry died in 1991, I went fishing with Dean once. It was sort of to keep the connection going.

Harry Gaines was one of the pioneer guides on the Kenai River and was a major influence on my developing a love for the river. Harry's ashes were spread on the river when he died in 1991, but this rock was placed on shore as a memorial.

After Harry died from cancer that year, a memorial service was held on the river and shore at the fish camp. Harry's ashes were spread in the river. However, later, Dean had a large commemorative rock installed at the edge of his land just feet from the river. I was not more than 100 yards from the gang of kids, but it was quiet. The rock is a large, gray hunk and it is probably only a dozen feet from the bluff overlooking the river. It is definitely within the distance where "Quarter Mile Harry" operated. The rock, which Reuben Hanke calls "Harry's Rock," is emblazoned with a marker that reads, "Harry Gaines, August 16, 1930-July 31, 1991. Laid To Rest In This Part Of The Kenai River, August 8, 1991. He Has Laid Aside Business and Gone A Fishin.'"

The river flowed past in its green glory under the bright sunshine of midday.

One of the running jokes about the Classic is that it never rains on the fishermen. It might rain during dinner the night before fishing. It might rain after the event is over. But it doesn't rain during the tournament. So it should have been no surprise to anyone when Junior Classic day dawned sunny.

Reuben Hanke helps clean the salmon caught by the kids participating in the annual Kenai River Junior Classic.

Kids were parceled out four to a boat, making it four to a guide. The guide services on the river volunteered their time. "They're in guides' hands," quipped Ricky Gease, the executive director of the Sportfishing Association.

One interested observer was R. W. Weilbacher, owner of RW's Fishing & Big Eddy Resort, whose company is right there next to Reuben's. RW had volunteered three boats, but he wasn't guiding. RW has been running his guide service for thirty-four years, though, and he has seen a lot of changes on the Kenai River.

There was a feeling-it-out period for guiding. There was the explosion of fishing attention. And lately, there had been the worries about the slowdown in king returns and the future. "The last two years haven't been up to par," RW said.

The good news for the kids was that the objective was not king salmon, but silver salmon, which had taken over the river for their first-run turn, plus the bonus of the even-year pink salmon run.

"There are humpies in there," Reuben said. "They're going to catch a lot of fish."

RW was out to spectate. "I think it's great for these kids," he said. "They love fishing. You get a smile on their faces. I've enjoyed watching this."

As always, no matter how slick and knowledgeable the guide, it was impossible to guarantee that every angler would catch a fish during the allotted 1 to 4 P.M. fishing time. They were going to try their darnedest. There was a two-coho limit for the first run, but the goal was to send one fish home with each kid if at all possible. Expertise and luck aside, the fish would be pooled and then divided up.

Shortly before 4 P.M. the boats began drifting in, setting in motion a high-speed, choreographed effort impressive in its efficiency. As the guide docked, each young angler stood up, held up a fish caught, had their picture taken, and then deposited the fish in a cooler. The cooler was carried by an adult from the boat to the weigh-in scale and then on to cleaning tables, where an assembly line of apron-wearing experts, from Reuben to past Sportfishing executive director Brett Heber, did the slicing and dicing as smoothly as if they were human Veg-O-Matics. The cleaned fish were placed in plastic bags and the process kept rolling.

Some of the kids had never fished in their lives before that afternoon. Some of them had fished in the Lower 48 before parents were transferred north to fresh military assignments. Some had experience fishing in Alaska or on the Kenai River, but not very much of it.

Coele Whaley, eleven, said this was her second fishing trip in Alaska. Ava White, ten, was spellbound as the men at the cleaning table cut open her salmon. "Is that the heart?" she asked as the innards were cut out and tossed into the river to a growing group of seagulls. "I went fly fishing once," she said. "This wasn't as hard to do as I thought."

Allison Gawrys, thirteen, said she had been fishing before, too, "like two times." This was better than her other trips. "The boat was really fast," she said. Looking at fish stockpiled in the chest at the rear of the boat and the way they still flopped around, she thought, "It's still living, in a dead way." While at first that sentence seems as if it might have been uttered by Yogi Berra, upon closer inspection, I believe the girl's thinking was dead on. If you have ever observed fish flopping after they have been caught and taken out of the water, her description is apt.

Carlie Benefield, eleven, had a little more fishing under her belt, including fishing for halibut on the ocean. While some kids didn't want to touch a fish's body because they thought it was gross, Benefield had no such hesitation. She brought in a silver salmon that weighed around eleven pounds. Some people kiss their first fish catch of the day out of thankfulness. Some kiss a fish for luck. Familiar with the old, odd phrase, "kiss a fish," Benefield did so. "I'm proud of it," she said.

Dylan Tow, fifteen, said he had been on the Kenai River before and it deserves his highest personal rating. "The Kenai River is awesome," he said. Tow got a fish and he knew where it was headed. "This is going to be dinner."

Reuben was right. Plenty of fish were caught. It was refreshing after the numerous shutout days in pursuit of king salmon to see silvers piling up. The only thing worse than taking a kid out fishing and getting skunked is taking a kid out fishing and getting skunked in the rain and cold. Luckily, none of those things happened this day.

Quinton Jackson, nine, was one of the newbies. He had never fished before anywhere, so it was all new to him. He caught a silver salmon, but being a little guy without the benefit of practicing use of the proper technique, Jackson ran into difficulties reeling his fish to the boat. "I couldn't get it up," he said. What happened? "I finally got it up." So, Quinton, do you like fish?

"No," he said. Do you like fishing? "Yes." Well, one out of two isn't bad. Maybe eating fish will grow on him as he grows.

For one day each year during the Junior Classic the guides are more like schoolteachers. They are the only adult in the room (or boat), with young pupils who are learning the subject matter. They are the authority figure, but are also supposed to show the kids a good time.

White-haired Rick Richardson, one of Reuben's guides, is one of the oldest guides on the Kenai River with thirty-five years of experience. He thinks the secret to making sure the youngsters have a good time, beyond catching fish, is basic. "You just try to keep them busy," Richardson said.

Kids don't differentiate between what kind of fish they catch as much as discerning adults do when they pursue silver salmon and feel that humpies get in the way. A fish is a fish is a fish to a kid. The score of the four young anglers that went out with Richardson read this way: Three humpies, one silver, and one Dolly Varden.

"Two of them caught two fish," Richardson said. "Some of them wanted to stay out longer and the others wanted to go in earlier."

Paxton Rosenbaum, thirteen, had fished before but was making his first visit to the Kenai River. He hooked a king salmon, although he didn't realize it at the time. "It's different," he said of the Kenai experience. "Pulling that fish, it was stressful. I needed a lot of help on it. I saw it and it went straight down." Bringing in a thirty-pound king is going to be work.

The fish cleaning went swiftly as kids carried their fish from the scales to the tables and then walked away with the cleaned fish in plastic bags. Sometimes the weight in the bags was too much for a smaller child to lug without throwing it over a shoulder.

One little girl came off the boat empty-handed and was inconsolable in the telling of what happened. Crying as she spoke, the girl told one of the Junior Classic organizers of the fish that got away. "It's just killing me," she said through her tears. "It's just killing me, Miss Susan. It got to the boat and floated away."

Whether the observation was literally true or not about it killing her, this girl seemed to be the only one who didn't catch a fish who really cared. As the event wound down, all of the kids were gathered together sitting on the lawn. Gease briefly addressed them by saying, "Did everybody have fun?" He got a big cheer in response. "That's all I wanted to know," Gease said.

Rick Richardson has been guiding on the Kenai River for thirty-five years, as long as anyone around, going back to a time before Alaska even licensed guides.

Miss Susan, aka Susan Doolittle, took over. "Who did not catch a fish?" she asked, though not looking for an answer. "Who cares? We're all a team. We're one group."

Doolittle was trying to figure out if enough fish were caught to share so that every youngster got a fish to bring home. A count was made of how many kids caught two fish, how many caught one fish, and how many didn't catch a fish. While the arithmetic was being computed the team was herded on to buses for the ride home.

The adults had about three hours to sort out the best way to give everyone a fish and make every kid happy before they exited the bus.

Organizers and guides tried to make sure every kid got a fish during the Kenai River Junior Classic.

FISHING WITH OLD MAN RIVER

I had been fishing with Rick Richardson before, more than once over the years. But one notable trip was in August of 2009, the first time daughter Alison and I took Malachi on the Kenai River. Britain was still too young to go.

For some reason grandson Malachi was pessimistic about catching a salmon. "I'm never going to catch a fish," he said at the start of a sunny morning that blossomed into a sixty-degree day. But he caught a silver and a king salmon that day. What he refused to do was actually touch the silver that was kept (the king was released since it was out of season). "I'm not going to hold a bloody fish," he said.

Richardson had long before come to understand that every kid going fishing was different from every other kid. He applied that knowledge in the Junior Classic, but he had stored the information away long before that.

"I've had an eight-year-old that I would hire as a guide," Richardson said. "I had a girl that caught a fish in two seconds. I also had a guy [an adult] on once who drank thirty-six beers and didn't have to go to the bathroom. And he didn't catch a fish."

Richardson's conclusion on Malachi, who was eight at the time, was: "He did better than I thought he would."

The day after the 2012 Junior Classic I joined Richardson in a boat with another fisherman named Jess Howard and his wife, Val, a couple from Calgary, Alberta. I was not a happy camper when informed I had to be ready to go by 5 A.M. "Are the fish really awake at that time of day?" I asked. I never got a straight answer.

We set out in pitch dark and Richardson had a light attached to a pole a few feet tall posted like a sapling on the front of the boat. I supposed it was intended to act as a warning to other boats like the way taller buildings have extra lighting on top to clue in pilots. The target fish was coho, or silvers. Bait was allowed and Richardson had a ready supply of salmon eggs. We didn't get very far when Richardson stopped the boat and removed a gas tank. "Uh, oh," Jess said. "Does this mean we have to paddle?" Fortunately, it did not. Richardson just switched out the tanks.

It was so quiet on the river it just supported my theory that everyone else was still asleep and even the fish were in a coma, so what were we doing out there so early? Well, the guide knows best, and if you don't believe that you shouldn't go out with a guide.

Richardson, sixty-five, is originally from Minnesota. But he had a brother-in-law who was an Alaska Bush pilot and he returned to the Midwest with stories about huge fish. Richardson, who has a voice as gravelly as the bottom of the Kenai River, was intrigued.

"I didn't even know what a king salmon was," Richardson said. He came north in 1974, worked in a cannery, worked construction, and worked as a deckhand on a commercial fishing boat for halibut. Then he became a guide on the river, and is still a guide, thirty-five years after first trying it.

Not only were a mere handful of people guiding when Richardson started out, the state didn't even have procedures in place to qualify, license, or test guides.

"If somebody paid you, you were a guide," Richardson said. "There were no licenses or anything."

There are now. With the popularity of king salmon fishing spreading and with more and more people setting themselves up as guides, the state did implement regulations to test and license guides, although the Coast Guard administered a river test. Richardson even helped develop the first test. When the process was completed, Richardson had Kenai River fishing guide license No. 1. "I still have that license," he said.

When he first tried Kenai guiding, Richardson only guided for two weeks, using vacation time from his job working in the taxidermy business. Then he joined Tex Dean, an early guide whose business had the motto "Fun Fishing With Tex." "Pretty soon I was guiding the whole season," Richardson said. "I didn't think I'd stay this long." Once, in the 1980s, Richardson was involved in guiding in an event for Tex that included 125 boats on the river. "I'm sure it's a record," he said.

The first salmon Richardson caught from the Kenai River was obtained while standing on the bank in Sterling. Given the way it was fighting, everyone watching said it was probably a thirty-pound king. Since the fish really weighed seventeen pounds that should have been a clue about the overly optimistic outlook of anglers. But for a guy who was used to focusing on walleye in Minnesota, it was a monster. "I thought that was the biggest fish in the world," Richardson said with a laugh.

Eventually, Richardson discovered what a true Kenai River monster really looked like. Some years ago he was fishing with his son and the lad caught an eighty-eight-pound king. "It didn't even fight much," said Richardson, who noted that the fish became a wall mount. The biggest king a client has caught with him weighed seventy-nine pounds and the biggest king he ever caught himself weighed seventy-five pounds. Those are all gargantuan fish.

About twenty-five years ago, he said, a friend of his caught a ninety-one-pound, ten-ounce king in Poachers Cove. They were cleaning some boats and when they finished decided to reward themselves with a short fishing jaunt. They made a couple of passes of the area and bingo, the fish struck. It was so strong that it broke the hook, Richardson said. "I netted it and it bent the net. The hoop collapsed. Right away we knew we had a big fish. There were three sets of hooks in him."

They rushed the fish to Ken's Tackle Shop in Soldotna for an official weigh-in, and whenever someone shows up to weigh a fish shoppers gather to watch. "A Japanese guy on the spot offered $4,000 for the fish on the hook," Richardson said. No sale was consummated, however. The fish got mounted.

The day was so nice for us that there was barely a hint of wind. While that enabled us to stay warm, it created perfect weather for mosquitoes and we were waving our hands in front of our faces more than a beauty queen.

Jess hooked a couple of fish in a row that were no longer fish. They were carcasses of spawned out salmon that were floating past. "Honey, stop catching those," Val said. "They aren't good eating."

We decided those were ghost fish. They couldn't open their mouths and grab a hook so they must have somehow magnetically made the connection. It was nearly 7 A.M. "OK, let's catch something that's still alive," Richardson said. "Something that's still flippin'." Sounded like a capital idea to me.

Richardson has blondish hair going white and Fu Manchu facial hair. He was wearing a camouflage shirt with chest waders decorated with yellow suspenders and a camouflage Harry Gaines Fishing hat. He was good company as we sought to entice fish.

In the late 1980s, Richardson had a ninety-two-year-old man out fishing for kings with him and he filmed the trip. "The guy never cracks a smile the whole time," Richardson said. Actually, for a while as a sideline, Richardson offered videos of entire fishing trips to clients. He did that for two years and business was quite good. He thought it would be an added attraction and for a while he couldn't keep up with the demand. Anyway, so on this trip a fifty-pound king was caught, but it was very difficult to subdue because the net broke in half. One guy in the boat beat on the fish's head with a thermos.

That was at the height of the Kenai River king salmon boom. There was fish for everyone. There were guides galore. Fishermen would be surrounded by other boats and could see lines popping left and right with fish on.

"The lines were going off all over," Richardson said. "I don't think we'll ever see that again. Not in my lifetime. I hope we do, but I don't think so." He paused. "All the guides I started with are dead."

A running joke started because of the ninety-two-year-old man and his son Bob. "Bob was always the last guy in the boat to catch a fish," Richardson said. "We called him, 'What about Bob?'" And that stuck for other fishing trips, with the joke being explained to someone who was the last one each time out to catch a fish.

Between all of the storytelling, Richardson was maneuvering the boat around to the best fishing holes on the Kenai. After one move we finally hit the right spot. A fish hit me in a fierce attack, bending the rod. I reeled and the fish fought. Got the salmon almost within reach of the net Richardson was holding over the side, and it spit the hook. The same thing happened to Jess soon after. Grr.

A few minutes later, boom! A nice silver was on. It felt like a heavyweight, but it came in steadily. It looked huge in the water. This one hung around and Richardson swiped the net across and we had this baby. "Nice goin', Lew," Val intoned. "That's a nice silver," Jess said. "They're all nice when they're in the boat," I said. Richardson deposited the fish in the box in the back and we could hear it banging around for a while.

Then Jess got a fish on. It splashed and resisted, but he reeled the fish in and on board. "Nice fish, honey," Val said. "We're not skunked."

A minute later Jess hooked another salmon. It splashed in the distance, and it too was reeled in. "You're showing off now, honey," Val said of his quick catch. Only this time it was a humpy and we didn't keep it. It had us fooled. They might not be as coveted or as tasty, but I've got to give humpies their due. They are a fighting fish, too, and when you hook one and reel, if you're a fisherman you're still having fun, and in many cases you don't know whether you have a silver or a humpy on. They generally weigh six or seven pounds. Granted, they don't match up well in the tale of the tape against a Chinook salmon, but they crush those panfish from the Lower 48 in head-to-head categories.

One after the other, I caught a humpy, Jess caught a humpy, and Val caught a humpy. I started thinking again that maybe the guides were missing out by disparaging the catching of humpies. They were in the river swimming right alongside those silvers. They bit as often as silvers. They fought like silvers. Maybe there is a future in humpy fishing for guides who will need the income if king salmon fishing remains moribund. I thought it was a keen idea and that I was helping to jump-start an entire industry. All the humpies need is an image change and a public relations campaign.

When we had another lull in the action Richardson told us the story about guiding a Texas oilman in the 1970s. The guy shows up on his boat and goes, "If you get me a sixty-pound king I'll give you a $500 tip." Well, that's not something a guide hears very often. But actually guides try to find fish for everyone and they never know how much they're going to weigh.

In this case Mr. Texas hooked a fish and it was a big one. It fought hard and so did the fisherman. "It came within six inches of the net," Richardson said, "and it snapped the line." Richardson had been using forty-pound test line and he promptly went shopping and bought eighty-pound test. "I bought eighty-pound test and I never lost another one."

Jess nailed another humpy. I caught a humpy. They seemed plenty aggressive and offered some entertaining battles. Richardson said some anglers keep one from a day's fishing. The nickname humpy for the pink salmon is applied because the fish have humps in their backs. Sometimes when a fisherman throws his line it sinks right into the big hump. That creates a tremendous war. It provides the human with the belief he has hooked a huge fish and it takes full-blown effort to reel it to the boat because it is not appropriately hooked. I was reeling and reeling. Val got one on at the same time. Richardson alternated his comments from "Attaboy" when he at first believed we had silvers on, to lack of interest when he realized we were expending tons of energy to reel in humpies.

Val was convinced she had a silver salmon on the line. Richardson informed her otherwise. "That's the biggest humpy I've ever seen," she said of a fish that might have weighed nine pounds. Then Jess got excited by a strike. It was a humpy dressed up as a silver.

Suddenly, Val got hot. She was reeling in humpies left and right. On about the third straight fish she hooked, she all-knowingly said, "Humpy." Only this time it was a silver. But it wasn't hooked well through the lips and it would take some deft handling not to lose it. Val very carefully led it up to the boat. She was backing up in the boat all of the time. Richardson grabbed it in the net.

"Good job all around," he said. There were high fives all around, too. From the net to the box for the fish and excitement from Val, but before she even caught her breath she had another fish on. This one got off the hook, though. Jess hooked a humpy through the dorsal fin and it seemed to be a big one.

Val and Jess were catching plenty of fish on their fourth day of Alaska fishing, making their journey from Calgary worthwhile. It's not as if Canada does not have its share of good fishing, though, so why travel a couple of thousand miles farther north?

"We knew about the Kenai River," Jess said. "It's one of the best places to catch salmon in the world. Growing up, it was always my dream to come salmon fishing in Alaska. Everybody always said that if you want some of the last best wilderness experiences you've got to go to Alaska."

Jess and Val Howard, avid anglers from Calgary, Alberta, fulfilled a lifelong dream with a fishing vacation to Alaska and the Kenai River and took home enough fish for many meals.

I have been to Calgary and it is a modern and somewhat large city, but I think of much of the rest of Canada as pretty wild. The Yukon Territory is very much like Alaska. The Northwest Territories has plenty of wilderness left. But that lure of Alaska, going back to the Gold Rush days of the 1890s, is apparently still strong in people's minds. When Jess told friends he was going to Alaska, they reacted suitably, saying, "Oh, you lucky bastard, that's the mecca."

Val and Jess had already been halibut fishing and they weren't done putting in their time on the Kenai River, either. They were boxing up fish to ship home wherever they stopped. At that point they had accumulated fifty pounds of halibut and fifty pounds of salmon, so they were going to make this vacation last. The fishing had been every bit as good as they had hoped. "If we limit out, it's more of a bonus," Jess said. "We're here making memories."

Jess got another bite. "That's a silver," he said. Maybe it was and maybe it wasn't and maybe it was gone. The fish wasn't pulling. "I think it eluded me," Jess said. "Rick, is he still there?" The fish jumped, with the hook still in his lips. "Oh yeah, he is," Richardson said.

Every once in a while one of us was fooled by a snag. We caught a rock, but were able to pull off the hook. We caught a branch and it felt like a good bite, but was a false alarm. Richardson told us about Beaver Hole, which was apparently the Kenai River's all-time snag. There might as well have been a redwood tree down there the way it ate lures. This was some time back, and the snag got on so many guides' nerves that as a group they decided something had to be done about it. With great effort and cooperation and the use of a truck as an aid, the log was removed, revealing the all-time treasure trove of stuff from under the water. "There were like 4,000 lures, lawn chairs, knives," Richardson said. "They put it on display at the Visitors Center. We took a lot of big fish there, but the aggravation was unbelievable. I found ten of my lures there, but everybody was hooking into it."

A fish hit Jess's line hard. "You've got a silver on," Richardson said. "It's a shark," said Val. It turned out to be a humpy. "I'm not cursing the fact I caught a fish," Jess said. That sounded like a prudent attitude. It was a big, fat humpy. Val insisted on taking a picture to show their kids. Married eighteen years they have two boys and a girl. Val was already writing the caption for the picture. "This is what we were throwing back, sons," she wanted to tell them. And it was true. Back in the river went the humpy, a salmon that probably weighed seven pounds.

My turn was next, reeling in a female humpy. As Richardson leaned forward to release the catch he grabbed the line instead of the net, and the fish spit the hook right at him and the sharp hook imbedded itself in his shirt. Luckily, he was well-armored and would not need to make an appearance at the Central Peninsula Hospital emergency room and be represented on the faux mannequin. "Lew," he said, "you're not supposed to catch the guide."

"Who's hand was on the line?" I replied.

I wasn't counting fish this day since the pace was fairly hectic, but Richardson said on a previous day with four people fishing they had humpies on their hooks constantly for an hour. "It was a humpyfest," he said.

On many occasions in a boat when the action was slow, I had been known to utter the phrase, "C'mon fish." Val took up a similar coaxing strategy, but she was more specific. "C'mon silvers," she said. "Don't be shy. Step right up to the boat."

Seemingly, they listened because Jess got a hit about one second later. "It's a dandy," he said. "Lew, it did work." Jess did a nice job of carefully reeling in a lightly hooked silver. This coho had some girth. "Come to momma," Val said. A few minutes later she had a silver on. Another good listener. Richardson looked at her and said, "Fish whisperer."

Since Val's tactics appeared to work, she started all over again. "C'mon silvers," she said. "Don't be shy." I've been a dummy all of these years addressing my remarks to fish in general rather than saying, "C'mon kings."

A request for a bathroom break was issued and Richardson even had a story about that. After thirty-five years on the river there's nothing he thought he hadn't seen, but this was a one-time occurrence. He climbed out of the boat at one of the boat launch areas on the river that had portable restrooms. There was only one problem—he got locked in. Someone was in the boat, waiting for him to come back, but was out of earshot as Richardson yelled for help. He shouted for fifteen minutes but no one responded and he didn't have the cell phone number of his client. Running low on options, Richardson did what he didn't want to do—he pulled out his cell phone and called the boss, Reuben Hanke, in his office, and relayed his predicament. Reuben's reaction was predictable. "You what?" he said.

Reuben hung up the phone and called Richardson's fisherman sitting in the boat wondering what happened to him. Once alerted the guy approached the port-a-john and pushed the door. The stuck bolt wiggled and Richardson was set free. The next day when he went out to his boat in the morning to guide he discovered some lovely gifts. One was a mini-paddle, in case he was ever up the creek again. Another was a screwdriver, a nice tool he would have been grateful to have to use on the door the day before.

The second round of humpyfest continued. Jess reeled in another pink. "Boy, we're pulling in some big, old suckers," he said. Val followed with another one. "Humpy, humpy," she said, as if it was a new mantra. "Humpies stop it, silvers only are allowed now." The listening connection must have failed because she reeled in another humpy.

Near shore we spied a mother duck and a group of recently born ducklings. They hugged the land and sometimes disappeared in the overhanging brush. They were using the environment for protection because the heavy concentration of eagles in the area did not live on fish alone and showed no mercy to the young ones.

"They're easy prey, sitting ducks," Richardson said, using the cliché. "One day you'll see a hen with twelve babies and the next day there'll be one."

While we were enjoying the heck out of catching salmon for hours that morning Richardson revealed a surprising fact about himself. "I don't eat salmon," he said. We all looked up and blinked. "I was doing 300 salmon a year when I worked in taxidermy and I got tired of it."

Not all pink salmon get released. The ones that are saved for the most part get canned. There is an industry for them. A few days earlier Jess and Val kept a humpy and barbecued it. How did it taste? "Awesome," Val said. Hmmm, more evidence that maybe I'm right and humpies will be the coming thing.

Another humpy, and another, and another for our friends from Calgary. "A couple of keepers," Val said. Visions of another barbecue were in their eyes. "Humpies are fish, too, you know," Jess said, as if he was about to start a Humpy Rights Movement. "Everybody puts humpies down."

If you hear about a Humpy Anti-Defamation League starting up in western Canada, you can probably figure that Val and Jess Howard are at the root of it.

KING SALMON NEWS

The king salmon *were* late. It wasn't as if the Kenai River was inundated, but the second run of Chinooks was stronger than the first run, which was somewhat heartening news. At least that was one way to look at it, even if there weren't tons of them.

The Kenai River fishing season for kings closed on the last day of July, but kings kept returning to the river past August 1. It's not as if the kings always follow the calendar, but they are usually more predictable in their return to the river to spawn.

Reuben Hanke pondered this information. "We ended up getting 30 percent of the second run after the first of August," he said. "Usually, it's 10 percent or so."

That still didn't provide much in the way of an answer as to what was going on, but it did mean there were more kings in the river than there had been in July. Normally, the early part of July produces a huge influx of kings at the start of the second run.

"I'm not saying it was a spectacular run," Reuben said of the late-arriving fish. "I've never seen it that dead during the first week in July. We got a late surge of kings. That's a good thing. There's still a lot of questions up in the air. Is there something big going on? Who knows? We're looking at fish from five or six years ago coming back from this spawning class. You can make tweaks and adjustments to the fishery, but you've got a long time seeing what the effects really are."

It was still early in the silver run, with weeks to go, and the early returns were encouraging. "The silver run seems pretty good," Reuben said. "At least it seems to be about average."

The king salmon season was over and Bob Penney was disturbed by what he saw.

"I couldn't take my kids fishing," he said. "I couldn't take my grandkids fishing. I could choose to live just about anywhere. But I live here by the Kenai River because that's where the king salmon are."

Penney didn't want to utter the phrase that was clearly on his mind. He could have said, "That's where the king salmon used to be."

By the end of August Alaska Fish and Game had an estimate ready on the 2012 king salmon return into the Kenai River. The report read this way: "Final Late Run Kenai River Chinook Inseason Summary. King salmon run update total was 21,817 fish. Based on historical run timing since 2002 the 2012 run was about eight-to-nine days later than normal, as approximately 36 percent of the run arrived after July 31. The cumulative catch per unit effort in the test netting program and the net-apportioned sonar indices were the lowest on record since 2002."

In 2005, 114,827 kings were counted as entering the Kenai River—if the count was accurate given the confusion that has arisen since about the positioning of the sonar. In 2011, a much slower year, 42,297 fish were counted as entering the river. Whatever the accuracy of those numbers, the count in 2012 was much lower.

Later in the Chinook report for 2012 the state indicated that it will develop a new escapement goal for 2013, meaning there might be some changes.

"The total run was probably one of the lowest ever," said Robert Begich, the area management biologist. "You can't point to one thing and say 'When we do this we'll have good king runs again.' It's very apparent there's a big change. We don't know exactly what it is."

That was the theme of the summer no matter who you asked.

Meanwhile, the lack of king salmon started making waves Outside. With people from all over the United States and the rest of the world coming to the Kenai River to fish in the summer, it was no wonder that the shortage of kings and the imposition of tough regulations to limit fishing garnered attention beyond Alaska's borders.

In early August the *Wall Street Journal* wrote a major feature that was headlined, "Royal Pain: Alaska Missing Its King Salmon." It should be noted that king returns were down all over the state, not only on the Kenai River, though that is the most famous Alaska place that is home to king runs. The lead paragraph on the story was, "The king-salmon population is crashing in Alaska, a disastrous development that is rippling through the state's tourism-dependent economy."

However, for some reason the *Journal* report said that the fish can measure up to 130 pounds, and when it comes to sportfishing that's simply wishful thinking. "It's not just a fish crisis, it's an economic crisis," Alaska Governor Sean Parnell said in asking the Obama administration to declare an official disaster for the Yukon River and Kuskokwim River, both in the Interior. Such a declaration was for commercial fishing, not sportfishing, but the king shortage in those places also drastically affected Alaska Natives in those regions.

It was crystal clear on the Kenai Peninsula that hotels, restaurants, and stores that are normally filled with customers in the summer high season lost business. That was all in addition to the revenue lost by shut-down guides for sportfishing and seasonal commercial fishery workers.

The king season was over and people were left to pick up the pieces and hope for better days in August and September and into October with fishermen chasing other kinds of salmon. There were more than a million sockeye, as usual, in the Kenai River, the pinks were back on their cycle for the first time in two years, and the silvers were running. There were still salmon to be had in the Kenai River, just not the monster Chinooks this season.

September

WOMEN'S KENAI RIVER CLASSIC

The Kenai River Classic, approaching the end of its second decade of existence, has never been closed to women anglers, but the majority of the participants and political honchos have been men. Someone had a "Hey, how about us?" thought and presto, a women's-only classic was created. The sixth annual Women's Kenai River Classic was set for the beginning of September, immediately after Labor Day.

If anything, the Women's Classic is discriminatory. No men allowed in the boats, except for guides. No men allowed at the pre-event dinner. Even Bob Penney was seen fleeing his own house an hour or so before dinner was served. Any male organizers of the event had their participation cut off when drinks were served as the seventy-five ladies began sipping white wine and anything else they wanted that was stronger. The same rules applied as if it was a junior high school sleepover. Guys, close the door on your way out. Ricky Gease, the sponsoring Sportfishing Association's director, gave a few women an educational boat tour of the river during the day and he was one of the last men out.

"It's got a two-fold purpose," Gease said of the Women's Classic. "There's an education component about the importance of Kenai River conservation and also women have been the biggest growing segment of the fishing population. There was no other comparable event for women to come together and network. It's part of the fund-raising, too. Since Ted Stevens passed away we have focused more on participation in terms of Alaska corporations. It works out great with users contributing to the conservation of the resource."

Part of the thinking behind the event was that women can love the Kenai River as much as men can. But this is not merely a fishing event. It has blossomed into a networking event where corporate and political higher-ups can mingle and exchange ideas from concern about king salmon to establishing business deals. The Women's Classic sort of parallels the old men-on-the-golf-links deal-making image of the past.

"Alaska has more female executives than most places," said chairwoman Kristen Mellinger. "Most of those coming are from Alaska, but there were a few coming from Outside. We really are a networking opportunity."

Of course, the Women's Classic is very much a fishing opportunity, too. Mellinger was about to enter her sixth classic. An angler for twenty-five years, she has become more and more passionate about the Kenai as the years passed. Originally, her Kenai trips were camping trips. Then they were in a travel trailer. Now she and her family have a cabin on the river.

The first year of the Women's Classic there were forty-nine participants. The limit was seventy-five in 2012 and Mellinger could foresee having a higher cap in future years. "We'll probably see what one hundred looks like," Mellinger said.

While having a good time with wine and food and fishing is a major part of the agenda, it was obvious to Mellinger that in light of the situation on the river revolving around king salmon there was going to be a lot of talk about conservation as the women fished for silvers.

"Conservation is going to be more and more important as time goes by," Mellinger said. "We're in danger of losing one of the world's last great resources."

Mellinger began talking about the king salmon as if it was an endangered species, like tigers, and how it might become important for humans to simply leave king salmon alone for a while. "As a resident of the river I would gladly give it up so future generations could experience what I have," Mellinger said.

As men of the human species departed the gathering place for dinner one by one and the arriving guests replaced them in the house, it was clear some women had come directly from their offices. They were dressed, not for a river trip, but in classy business suits and dresses. They hadn't time to change as they traveled from Anchorage or elsewhere to the Penney residence.

The women brought different levels of fishing experience and different numbers of years of experience with the Classic to Soldotna. Natalie Lowman of Conoco Phillips, the oil company, was making her Classic debut. "We're really interested in salmon habitat protection," said Lowman, who is from Anchorage. She comes from a commercial fishing family and has worked in that profession since she was a teenager. Lowman has been ocean fishing for coho salmon and has fished the Kenai for silvers, too, so her background includes several aspects of Kenai Peninsula fishing. "Silvers are my favorite fish," she said.

Nadja Hipszer lives in Anchorage now, but she is originally from Switzerland, one of the places regarded among the most scenic countries on earth. Still, she rates the Kenai River pretty highly, too, for its beauty. "How could this river not pass the test?" she said.

Hipszer and her family spend a fair amount of time on the river fishing for kings, reds, and silvers. They usually go dip netting to fill the freezer for winter, as well, but not in 2012. "We're not well stocked because we didn't go dip netting. We only have a half-dozen to a dozen fish."

In the winter she said she walks along the river. "It's very beautiful," Hipszer added. "It's very pristine."

Terri Good, an Anchorage public relations woman, noted that many Alaskans refer to Mount McKinley, the 20,320-foot sentinel of the Alaska Range that is the tallest mountain in North America, as "The Great One." That is the translation of its native name, *Denali*. But using another definition, of a place in the state that deserves signature attention, Good said the Kenai River "to me is the Great One."

I had never heard that argument made, but for those who regard the Kenai as something uniquely special, it's understandable. There is nothing like McKinley anywhere else on the continent and to those who love the Kenai River there is nowhere else like it anywhere.

Good, who has participated in the Women's Classic every time it has been held, is enamored of the river for several reasons. "Just the peace," she said.

But it wasn't just peace that attracted her. There were several other reasons. "The magnitude of it," Good said, "and the beauty."

Good believes the Women's Classic has also matured into something more meaningful than a fishing tournament, as people outside of the event might think.

"It's not just about the fishing," she said. "It's about the opportunity to build relationships with the women. You're not at a stuffy cocktail party. What a location. They obviously care about the river." Good's lament is familiar to a lot of guys who admit that work often gets in the way of fishing time. "If I could, I would fish all the time," Good said. A motor home takes her to the Kenai as often as possible in the summer, and if nothing else the Classic does provide the chance to fish for silvers.

"How cool is it to be out on the river," Good said. Then her competitive instincts kicked in. There are prizes for the most fish and poundage and biggest, the typical categories where winners are rewarded in fishing tournaments. The grand prize is a Waterford crystal bowl. "Actually, it's all about the bowl," Good kidded. "I hope I catch a big one. I need a fish."

Don't we all.

The calendar still read summer and it was still in the nineties in parts of the Lower 48, but Alaskans with a sense of perspective understand that early September is really the middle of fall in Southcentral. Autumn is pretty much a blip on the radar screen rather than a true season in these parts. Blink and you miss it. Autumn is probably three or four weeks long in terms of what anyone reared elsewhere below the Arctic Circle thinks.

It was full-fledged fall on the Kenai Peninsula. Trees were changing colors and shedding leaves quickly. There were bright yellows and some reds among the leaves still clinging to branches. Green was fading fast. There was a crispness to the air, especially in the mornings, that definitely heralded the change of seasons. This was not just see-your-breath crispness, but approaching-freezing crispness. It was in the thirties for the start of fishing, although the sun broke through and warmed the air somewhat by lunchtime.

On the first of two days of fishing, eighteen boatloads of women caught thirty-eight silvers. The finale was Saturday, when fish catches were totaled and prizes, many of them made by Tiffany's, were presented. When the boats docked at the Harry Gaines fish camp, pretty much the same procedure was followed as was used during the Junior Classic. Women posed for pictures holding up their fish. The fish were taken to a scale, and then to a cleaning table, and ultimately returned to the women. As an illustration of the reduced role of men in the program, although his property was being used, Reuben Hanke was nowhere to be seen. He was off in another part of the state at hunting camp. His wife, Kelly, who works for the Sportfishing Association, oversaw much of the operation.

Once the initial pose-with-your-fish pix were taken, the keeper silver salmon were delivered to Dave "Wahoo" Cole, the official weigh master. The very first fish tipped the scales at 8.1 pounds, a respectably sized silver.

Fresh off the river came Hipszer, rubbing her hands together because they were cold. She collected a silver in mid-morning, but she said any momentum gained in the fishing hole was lost because all of the women in the boat "had to go potty" afterward because they had been drinking so much coffee.

On the first day of fishing, Hipszer thought she had hooked a real prize. "It was a big fight," she said. "I hooked it in the back and it took fifteen minutes to bring in." It was also a humpy, not a silver. Until the sun came out the women were pretty cold on board that boat, but she raved about the Women's Classic. "It was a fabulous experience," she said, proclaiming her intention to enter every year. "Why would I miss this?"

Fish were rolling in and being hauled to Wahoo. "Do I have to hold it?" asked Maureen Moore. "Are you kidding?" he said. "It breaks all my rules," she said. "I don't ever touch the fish. I love to eat them, though." Her silver was going to provide a meal or two for sure after weighing in at nine pounds.

Sherrill Miller looked like a potential big winner. In September, the limit on silver salmon rises to three per person per day from two and Miller caught silvers that weighed in at 9.3, 6.6, and 6.6 pounds. She had also limited out the day before with a big catch of 10.1 pounds. "That's a first," Miller trumpeted. "It's the first year I've limited out both days. It was awesome."

In 2011, Miller was the runner-up in total poundage caught. Things were looking pretty good for her in 2012, too. "That was a good haul," she said of the day's catch. "Sometimes it doesn't even matter if you don't catch fish. It's just fun to be with these guys. It's a good time. It's phenomenal."

Tara Sweeney made her way to the scale and watched intently as Wahoo adjusted the balance and made the big announcement: "13.2 pounds!" Whoa,

Sherrill Miller limited out with three salmon during the Kenai River Women's Classic two days in a row and caught a 10.1-pound silver.

that's a big one. Tara thrust her arms in the air and screamed. "Nice fish!" everyone shouted to her. "Thank you," she shouted back.

It took Sweeney ten minutes to reel in the husky silver and that was plenty of time to wonder if it was going to reach the boat or spit the hook. At one point the fish soared from the river and showed itself and Sweeney was convinced it was going to break free of her line then. "I was worried," she said. For Sweeney, this was a special catch because it was her first time on the Kenai River, the first fish she caught on the river. Later, she added a 7.9-pound silver, as well.

Sweeney may not have had much experience with catching her own salmon, but she knew what to do with the chunky fella. "It's going to be smoked," she said.

One of the most popular entrants in the Women's Classic each year is Jackie Purcell. She is a likeable enough lady, but her popularity is due to her career. Purcell has been the face of the weather report on Channel 2, the most-watched TV station in Alaska, for years. Mellinger, the chairwoman of the Women's Classic for the last two years, made a point of noting that it had never rained on the event. Purcell gets the credit and laughs about that, especially since TV weather reporters frequently take a lot of grief for having predictions go wrong.

"They think I have some superstitious power," Purcell said. That's because you talk to the weather gods all of the time, she was informed. "Exactly." Right then a man wandered up to Purcell, said hello, and said "Thanks for the great weather again." Purcell crossed an index finger and middle finger and said, "Yep, me and Mother Nature, we're like this."

Purcell said her reputation began building and she began accumulating goodwill at the Women's Classic the first year when it was supposed to rain and didn't. She was late arriving and her timing coincided with the weather clearing. Not that Purcell needs to have balmy weather to fish on the Kenai. She loves the river and shares her passion for it with her husband, Daniel Pearson. They have fished on the river many times in their fourteen years of marriage, but about four years ago they started celebrating their anniversary each year with a trip to the river for getaways.

"I just feel like I'm happy when I'm on the river," Purcell said.

And that's despite the fact that she suffered a fishing injury when hauling in the biggest king of her life, a fifty-three-inch Chinook. When the fight with the king was over, Purcell being the winner, she noticed a throbbing in her thigh. She had a huge bruise and figured out it was from the pole pressing against her leg as she battled the brute. "It was my fish bruise," Purcell said. It was small price to pay for a grand king salmon.

There were thirty silvers caught on the second day of the Classic, making a two-day total of sixty-eight. Sure enough, Sweeney's 13.2-pound baby was the biggest of them all.

After Good came off the river and warmed up a little in the now-pleasant sunshine, she was asked if she had fun. "Of course, I did," she said, and that was despite not catching any fish on Day 1. Good more than made up for that by catching a 10.9-pound silver quite early in the morning on Day 2.

"I caught it right away," she said, when it was still in the thirties and her feet were freezing. "I didn't know I had a fish on. It came in easily. It was nice looking, but I didn't think it was that big. I caught two fish and I was sure the other one was bigger."

For Good, the Kenai River sightseeing was as special as the Kenai River fish catching. From the boat her group saw a bear with two cubs and eagles all around. "We are so lucky to live in Alaska," she said. "I've gotten skunked and it hasn't diminished my love of the Kenai. Another great weekend."

HANGING WITH THE OTHER MR. FENTON

As a basic reminder of where I was, the hotel in Soldotna where I spent the night had fish-design carpeting. There were fish in red, fish in green, and fish in the color of the Kenai River. I wouldn't have minded one of those rugs myself, but I don't know if it's for sale at the average Wal-Mart.

This time I was fishing the Middle River for silver salmon with Murray Fenton as my guide, the other half of the brother tandem in Fenton Brothers. I was giving equal time to him after fishing with sibling Mike the previous month. It was me and a crowd of other guys, Derek DeYoung from Montana, his father, Gordy DeYoung from Michigan, and Bob Sizemore from Soldotna.

Although the fishing was improved over the dismal king salmon season, the silver salmon season wasn't exactly overwhelming anyone at the moment. "It hasn't been stellar, but this sort of has mirrored what has been going on," Murray Fenton said as he motored the boat into the first hole of the day, one that was a little bit warmer at forty degrees.

With the lines bobbing nervously on the bottom and making the fishermen nervous, or at least fooling them into believing they had a bite, the others inquired how they would know for sure when a fish bit. "You'll feel them when they get on," Fenton said. "You've got to give them a little jerk, then keep the line tight."

While most of us were using salmon rods provided by Fenton Brothers with thirty-pound test, Gordy wanted a different challenge. He brought his own rod and had ten-pound test line on it. We all used artificial lures. Our biggest worry when we first started out was the wind. It was annoyingly strong. "There have been times I've just been beat up by it," Fenton said. "Hopefully we're not going to be fishing in a hurricane," Bob said.

Derek had the first catch of the day—a humpy. Apparently those guys were going to be a factor as we tried to focus on silvers. Gordy held the fish up in the air and chanted, "Humpy, humpy, humpy. Smile when you say it."

Murray Fenton and his brother Mike have operated Fenton Brothers guide service on the Kenai River for a quarter of a century and they both have had their share of adventures.

It started raining a little bit, but not hard enough to soak through our clothing. That's one thing I always hate, getting drenched through supposed protective rain gear with my trusty notebook getting soaked through to ruination. I was once out on a river in Illinois and it just poured on us. I don't remember what kind of fish we were catching, or even if we caught any. All I remember is the aftermath, sloshing back to my hotel room, peeling off every single item of clothing. I then spread out the clothes all over the floor, took out my notebook and peeled apart each page, unsticking the pages, and then turned the heater up full blast and left the room. I've only had to go to that extreme a couple of times, but I was hoping this day didn't represent a third such situation.

"This is how I get my shower every day," Fenton said. Heh, heh. I hoped he was joking. The good news was that the rain quickly turned to a light drizzle and then stopped. Whew. One by one we hooked humpies and brought them to the boat. The guys had a good attitude about it. They decided we should write a country song about humpies. "Humpy By the Trail" was the first suggestion, though I was not sure what that meant.

Derek was a catching machine. He made picturesque casts, the whooshing, whippet sound unmistakable. More than ever I was convinced humpies ruled the Kenai River this summer. "It's insane," Fenton said, mentioning a recent angler who caught fifty of them on one fishing trip. Derek kept hooking humpies until he finally stopped to catch a breath. "That was fun," he said. "They're crowd pleasers in a way," Fenton said.

Another defense of humpies was spelled out by Bob. "The thing humpies are good for is teaching people how to fish," he said. "That's how we taught our kids how to fish." Interesting thought, humpy fishing as an educational tool, and why not since they were so abundant an angler repeated his casts, his reeling, and all other style forms while bringing them into the boat, whether they were worthy of being kept or not.

The year before the Kenai River was running with higher water than usual during the second silver run and Fenton said he had to use some ingenuity to find the fish. He steered the boat into a back channel rarely fished on the Middle River. This channel, naturally, was not nearly as wide as the main river, so when a grizzly sow and two cubs showed themselves on shore, Fenton paid attention. His clients busied themselves taking photos, but he was eyeing the way out of the channel. One angler got a fish on and was fighting it. That's when the bear took note of the boat and how close it was. The mother bear raced out of the woods and into the water, flying at them lickety split as Fenton fired up the engine for retreat.

"We were all kind of freaking out," he said. The angler with the fish on still had it hooked and as the boat picked up speed, his hook and line kept dragging the fish with them. "The bear watched us leave. She was between a nine- and ten-foot bear. She was very aggressive. Her attitude was, 'Get the hell out of here, this is my fishing spot.'"

Although in my summer experience the bears were hidden from view, they are definitely a hazard of the terrain, and someone like Fenton, who goes out on the water five days a week for months, is almost guaranteed the occasional run-in.

"We've had them at Bings Landing," Fenton said of the popular put-in location for boats and one particular tale from September of the year before came to mind. "A guy launched his boat and he looked up and a bear was standing right there on the dock looking at him."

"That will make you change your shorts," Bob said.

The good news was that the sky grew brighter, the sun began warming us, and the light on the river made it as beautiful as it ever looks. The new-to-the-Kenai anglers were happy to be there. Derek said he had been thinking of a Kenai River salmon trip for seven years. Gordy said, "It was on my bucket list. It's been well worth the wait." Bob is the one who made it happen. He was traveling through Livingstone, Montana, and happened upon Derek's gallery. They struck up a conversation and Derek said he always wanted to fish in Alaska with his father. Some time passed, but Bob invited them and here they were on their dream trip.

The trip was a bigger picture than just the Kenai, with a fly-in to Crescent Lake, the raved-about location used by the Kenai River Academy organizers, and a halibut fishing journey, as well. Bears were seen, moose, eagles. "It was like *Jurassic Park* without the dinosaurs," Gordy said.

At Thompson's Hole we saw an eagle and looked up and saw others on the way. Fenton had actually seen bears at the same place the day before. Derek is an artist who actually paints fish, though it is a toss-up whether he would rather make art of the ones in his head or catch the ones at the end of a hook. Derek cut through the humpies to hook a silver. It was a big one and a fighting one and when he reeled up to the side of the boat we all got a look at it and were impressed. "That's a silver bullet right there," Bob said. "I was beginning to think they didn't like me," Derek said. "That's a beauty," Fenton chimed in.

Much oohing and ahing followed. "That's a great fish," Bob said. Numerous pictures were taken of the captured silver. "All right," Derek said. "That was neat." The only one who looked unhappy was the fish. "Look at the big nose on that baby," Bob said. Gordy guessed its weight at twelve pounds. The chatter kept up about that silver, which was still bebopping around in the box, flopping its body in heaves. Then it grew quiet. "He's dead," Derek said. "But he's slippery," Gordy said.

Gordy took some ribbing about his light tackle. "You've got your four-pound test," Derek teased. "It's a piece of string." Every once in a while father and son teased each other and Bob and I were in the cross fire. Gordy put a hook into a humpy, but with his light line it was no easy task to reel it in. As he worked the fish the line was once again derided, this time labeled dental floss. Worse, Gordy hooked it in the hump, not the lips, so the fish was zooming all over the place, pulling hard.

The choice was made to net this humpy and keep it for cooking. Bob volunteered to handle the net, but the fish was so lightly hooked it took us for a ride as Gordy determinedly kept it on and sought to bring it closer to the side. Bob lowered the net into the water, but the fish had other ideas and zipped right past it. Gordy got on Bob's case for missing it and Bob responded, "It was going by at ninety miles per hour." More reeling, the humpy moved back into our area code and Bob leaned over again, and he missed netting it again. "It was going 100 miles per hour and leaving a wake," Bob said.

"I'm wearing him out!" shouted Gordy. Wearing the humpy out that no one else even wanted, as Bob observed, and added that the entire episode was eating up a half hour of fishing time for everyone else.

Gordy reeled the humpy in once again and rather than have Bob net it, Fenton released it. I got splashed in the face as it disappeared. "Welcome to my world," Fenton said. I was about to volley him a snappy comment in return when something hit my rod. It didn't feel like a full-fledged bite, but it made me pay attention. "There's something fishy with my rod," I said. Sometimes fish will play with the hook, sniffing around it, studying it, pondering whether it's worth taking a bite. There was no harder hit this time. No go.

We were busy little campers because of the humpies even if we were after silvers. The silvers, like the kings, did not seem to be as plentiful this year. Of course, they weren't as scarce either. There have been times when a guide like Fenton could take out four fishermen like us and have everyone catch their three-fish limits in an hour or so, or at the least have the fish on board by quitting time at midday.

"We used to get limits every day," Fenton said, "and it was unusual not to get them. This year it's unusual to get a limit."

Bang, bang, bang, I had a hit, Bob had a hit, and Gordy had a hit, three in a row, three men reeling at once, three fish on and coming in to the boat, creating a bit of a frenzy on board. They were all humpies, of course. "We must have gone through humpy hell," Bob said. "Or maybe it should be called humpy heaven," I said. "Maybe we should have targeted humpies to see how many we could get." None of us had any idea how many fish we had caught, but it was a bunch, certainly twenty-something, maybe thirty-something fish. Derek laughed at the notion of focusing on humpies, but got into the spirit of the idea. "Then the silvers would be the bycatch," he said. A moment later, Derek joined us by picking up the fourth humpy within minutes.

As soon as he let it go, a fifth took over Derek's hook, as if it had been waiting in line to take a turn. Gordy got another fish on, but this one was a tough guy and it broke his light line clean off. That had to happen at some point on this day with Gordy tempting fate as he had. "I never saw a humpy jump like that," Bob said of the big one that ripped apart Gordy's tackle. "Was it a humpy?" Fenton asked. We all assumed so at first, given how many we had been catching, but Bob thought about it and said, "I don't know."

We could barely keep up with the humpy bite and became so used to them that every hit we got had to prove it was another kind of fish to elicit any excitement from us. Bob got a fish on that purchased our attention, though, and it really got everyone excited when we finally saw it. He reeled in a twenty-six-inch rainbow trout that was more spectacular than any rainbow we had ever seen in the sky. Its body might as well have been decorated with a Crayola box. "That's a monster," Gordy said in admiration. Bob said, "That's a pretty good fish, isn't it? I told you they were in here." That was a little sexier bycatch.

The weather kept changing up on us, going from sunny to cloudy, from calm to breezy. At times it got fairly cool and at times we were pleasantly warmed. Bob got another rainbow trout on and it was jumping and splashing in the distance, looking like the most exuberant fish in the world. "It's Sizemore's day today," Gordy said. "Look at that thing. That is a football." Bob maintained his cool. "It's a really good fish, isn't it?" he said. Yes, sir, it definitely was a beauty. When rainbow trout are viewed up close their bodies show why they are so desired. Rainbows leave men drooling the way they do over a beautiful woman. Maybe they have some things in common, too, being usually unattainable and since the rainbows are also usually catch and release, both are hard to hang on to.

Over the approximately twenty-five years I have been fishing on the Kenai River, considerable development has taken place. There are more fancy homes and real estate values have skyrocketed. In 2012, though, it seemed as if there were more homes for sale than I had ever seen before, many of them gorgeous places that seemed far too beautiful to be used only seasonally, although I was assured most of them were just that. I was surprised by how many for sale signs we passed and I eventually looked up prices on them. There might have been a wide selection available, but it wasn't because they were being foreclosed. Their owners wanted top dollar and all of the ones I checked on had six-figure price tags, and not the low six figures either.

Not every property was jaw-droppingly gorgeous, and not every property was new. There are some homes overlooking the river on tiny lots of land and they look very vulnerable to flooding. There are also some houses that were clearly built just for summer weekend use with the barest of essentials. And finally, there were some mini-homes that seemed abandoned, or at least in serious disrepair. One tiny red building appeared not to have been touched in years. It loomed right above one of Fenton's favorite fishing holes, so he saw it often. "They've really let this go," he said.

That fishing hole was not a place Fenton invested time in for king salmon, but it was a productive one for silvers and rainbow trout in the fall, he said. As soon as he said it, Gordy got a hit and reeled in a rainbow trout. A small one, not nearly as impressive as the others we brought in. "You were saying," I said to Fenton. "Right on cue," he said. It was almost like a trained fish, taught to bite a hook the moment Fenton introduced it.

Although few people that I had run across wanted to stockpile humpies, Fish and Game did establish a limit just in case. You couldn't take more than six in a day. Someone suggested keeping them and smoking them. See, I knew all the humpies needed was a good marketing agent, to tell Alaskans and the rest of the world it is not a trash fish the way many in the United States view carp.

Since he is a local resident, Bob knows a lot of people in the area and that included people with property overlooking the river. One winter day he had permission to fish a slough in front of someone's house and was able to park his vehicle on their property. There was no other way to access the fishing spot he hiked his way into. It was cold and snowy, but he knew there were rainbow trout to be caught.

As he finished his good day of fishing, however, Bob looked up and there was a bear that hadn't had the common sense to hibernate yet. Bob looked at the bear and he looked at his car. The car wasn't far away, but neither was the bear. He stood still, trying to calculate whether or not he could reach the car before the bear reached him. Then he got a genius of an idea.

He delved into his pocket, pulled out his keys, and pressed the car alarm button. Waaa, waaa, waaa, it sounded loudly, startling the bear. Not that the bear moved far away, but it did move enough for Bob to scootch into the car safely. When Bob pulled away, the bear was comfortably settled at the side of the road.

Derek, who seemed to pick up the pace of his catching as the day wore on, hooked another fish. "That looks troutish," Bob said of the way it moved in the water. It was, but not one that came close to measuring up to the twenty-six incher.

We saw no bears that day, but by the time we quit in the afternoon we had seen a lot of fish. We caught humpies by the dozen, a handful of silver salmon, a couple of Dolly Varden, too, and those rainbow trout. "The football rainbow," Bob reminded us. In all, the general consensus was the boat caught about fifty fish. That's a good day no matter who is counting.

I had been on the Kenai River many, many times and Bob had been out on the river many more times than I had. For Gordy and Derek, father and son, it was a first, but they had no complaints. They would always remember the Alaska trip that finally became reality. They had a good haul of fish and were headed back to Bob's house to cook some for dinner. I was pretty sure that a humpy would make it onto the grill.

KENAI COMMUTERS

"As often as we can," said Kim Killion.

That was the summer game plan for Kim and her partner, Jenny Davis, who live and work in Anchorage about 160 miles away, but own a splendid house overlooking the Kenai River that I would take in trade for any city condo in the world. They have a canal that runs behind the house that leads directly onto the river about 100 yards away. Sweet deal all around.

They love fishing and what better place to hang out than the Kenai all summer long for weekend getaways? It looked like a dream set-up to me. They had a boat similar to the guide boats, berthed right out the back door and reposed in the three-and-a-half feet of water in the canal. It took about two minutes or so to get out on the river to get after the fish.

"It couldn't be better," Kim said of the cozy housing development fourteen miles from the mouth of Cook Inlet.

Many people refer to summer homes on the water as the family cabin, but calling this house a cabin was too facile a summary. Their friendly black dogs, one an adult lab and the other smaller and younger, shared the house, and there was ample guest room. I thought Jenny said they had it for ten years, but I didn't even think the development that had grown up since I had started fishing the river was that old. "It makes it really nice," Jenny said.

It was heading on to late Saturday afternoon on a sunny, clear day, so we thought we'd take a spin on the river to fish for a couple of hours before dinner. The target, as usual, at this time of year, was coho salmon. The obstacle, as it had been for the last month or so, was catching humpies instead.

"We'll try to drop into a spot other than where the humpies go," Kim said. Jenny praised the weather. Kim wanted to drive the boat. With no hat on and sunglasses filtering the brightness, the wind ripped through her hair and she looked like a professional guide. "I love driving the boat," she said.

Kim and Jenny are so passionate about fishing, and so regularly catch fish with the friends they invite out, that they have been asked many times if they haven't considered becoming guides. Jenny said she thought about it, but realized then the fishing would be work and she would rather it remained an avocation. They had been having pretty good luck catching silvers this season and only the week before Jenny brought in a fourteen pounder. That's a good silver.

"That was an epic battle," she said. The fish had the strength to haul her all over the river and it took some time to land as Jenny tried to reel and Kim tried to use the boat's power to advantage. "It was like the *Beverly Hillbillies*," Kim said of how it must have looked if anyone else was watching the whole show.

Kim grew up in Wyoming and came to Anchorage as a student and athlete at the University of Alaska Anchorage. She played basketball and volleyball for the Seawolves and it wasn't until she used up her eligibility that she started fishing the Kenai River in the mid-1980s, or at least as she put it, she began fishing it hard-core. "When I first went out I found out I had a lot to learn," she said. "I was born and raised in Jackson, Wyoming, and I only fly fished. I guess the neat thing about fishing on the Kenai is you learn something every single time."

Kim isn't kidding about learning more about the Kenai all of the time. In their river house the bible is really the annual tide book. Copies are kept within easy reach at all times. Not to mention the annual ritual they have when hosting a welcome-in-the-next-year party. "We hand out the brand-new tide books on New Year's Eve," Jenny said.

Cohos are her favorite salmon to fish for, Jenny said, more so than the more publicized kings. "I love the fight," she said. "It's a wonderful gift to be able to play a fish and the silvers give you an incredible rush. I love to fish for reds, too." They are able to do their subsistence fishing from the boat. "King fishing is just a lot of time," she said, echoing those Fish and Game statistics about the many hours needing to be devoted to catch kings. Jenny's most recent king catch of a thirty-five pounder dated back two years.

Jenny is not a native Alaskan either. She came to Anchorage in 1983 with the army and was stationed at Fort Richardson. She is now a civilian employee at the base. "The first salmon I ever caught was at the confluence of the Moose River and Kenai River," she said, taking note of that rite of passage in becoming a full-fledged Alaskan. "I don't think I even fished for a king until 1987 on a guided trip."

The boat was acquired in 2001, but just because she became a boat owner didn't mean she was instantly a first-class boat driver or knowledgeable fishing woman. Time was invested to master the skills needed to drive it and to gain awareness of the best places to fish on the river. "It took a long time to get the boat set up and to learn how not to look like a dork on the water," Jenny said.

That was a colorful way to put it, but that comment was also a useful information imparter for boat buyers. You may have the boat in your possession, but it doesn't imply because you launch it you know what you're doing without practice. It's not as if Jenny is putting down king fishing, either, because she has been part or party to the collection of some major-league Chinooks. The funny part is after announcing how long it took to really take charge of the boat with know-how, Jenny said that she wasn't out in the water for more than ten minutes with a friend when they hooked and landed a fifty-eight pounder.

Around 2009, Jenny and Kim went out fishing at Mud Island with the neighbor from the development, a guy named Ron, and another person, and they brought in a fifty-five pounder. "One thing about Ron is he doesn't leave any later than four in the morning," Jenny said.

Doesn't anybody believe in nighttime fishing under the midnight sun, so you can rise at a civilized hour? I have always wondered about this whole aspect of fishing. Why the early morning stuff? I thought it was the early bird who caught the worm, not the early fish. Not everyone was perky at such an early hour, but when Jenny's rod went off like an alarm clock, Ron was the first to react. "Get the blankety blank rod out of the blankety blank rod holder," he shouted. Jenny had difficulty pulling the rod out and grasping it, but managed without losing the king.

"It was an epic battle," she said, apparently using that as a common denominator description for the biggest fish she has brought in after a struggle. "It was pretty exciting. I never saw it until it got tired. Man, when I first saw it, it was something."

It was a pleasant afternoon to fish and Kim and Jenny seemed confident of the fishing hole chosen to focus on. As we held steady, we saw some competition off to the side. It was a seal, making its way from the ocean through Cook Inlet to the Kenai River in order to swipe our salmon. Every once in a while its black head popped up above the water's surface. Then it took a dive and reappeared maybe fifty yards in a different direction, the head bobbing along again.

We were using dried salmon eggs for bait and sometimes if a fisherman is not quick enough setting the hook a fish will strip the bait, leaving an empty, forlorn hook hanging in the water without the angler even knowing it. Thus one is wise to periodically check the status of the bait, and when Kim did so she realized with minor disgust that she had no idea how long she had been fishing with a bare hook. "That's what we call fishing on credit," Jenny said. "Just shut up and catch fish," Kim replied. "You guys are doing all the work."

That is, if you want to call hooking a salmon, reeling and watching it splash and slowly, but steadily come your way, work. There are occasions when it is difficult to bring in a big fish and there are occasions when muscles ache from reeling, but I have never heard anyone sitting in an office say they prefer their paperwork to fishing work.

While all of this banter was going on and Kim was moving the boat, parking the boat, and setting an anchor, I was catching silver salmon. After so many recent river visits when humpy were pretty much the boss fish of

Jenny Davis, a summer weekend commuter from Anchorage to the Kenai River, has become so expert at catching salmon that friends say she should become a guide.

the trip, I made no claims when I got my first hit. In fact, Jenny was the first to comment that I had a fish on. The hook was set, the pull on the other end was significant, and as I reeled I knew I had a good-sized fish on, but couldn't tell if it was a silver or a humpy.

I drew attention from both women (not a phrase I have uttered many times in my life) as the fish came closer, but was still hidden underwater. This fish was coming in, but it was a question of what kind of fish this was. There was some long-range splashing, but I still wasn't sure of the make and model. Jenny was coaching me. "Move up," she said. "Move back. Reel down." The ladies wanted that fish in the boat just as much as I did.

Finally, as a little scramble ensued with me reeling, the net being readied and the boat being steadied, the fish revealed itself as a silver for sure. Yep, a chrome-sided, picture-perfect salmon that was going to weigh in at around ten pounds. Yeah, baby. Kim scooped the fish up in the net and we had him. Now that the fish was captured and under lock and key I could exult. No premature celebrations with fish since so many spit the hook at the boat.

I thanked the ladies for their help and said they worked well as guides between finding the right spot, maneuvering the boat, and wielding the net. "We're a lot cheaper, too," Jenny said. "And we're always worth a good laugh."

Eagles were back, too. There were three in a tree right in front of us that seemed almost close enough to reach out and touch. The birds probably resented my catching a silver, so I don't know what they thought when I did it all over again a few minutes later. Fish on! Here we go again. This fish took the hook hard and it didn't get much chance to wiggle around and set the agenda. I was reeling and making progress from the start and I was the one in charge. Only a couple of minutes later I had the fish at the side of the boat and it was scooped up. Silver salmon No. 2 was ours, this one weighing about nine pounds. Jenny and Kim acted as excited as I felt about the dual catch, and I presented them with the fish. They would make better use of them cooking at the river house than I could have. I would have had to transport them a fair distance without a proper container and without a good way to keep them fresh.

The whole world seems beautiful when you go fishing and catch fish and the sun is out and the company is good and the water is inviting. It was one of those freeze-it-on-film days. This was one of those reminders of why it is so easy to love the Kenai River. All of the elements were in place for the perfect fishing trip and this was a kind-of-whim, two-hour journey. Throw in the wildlife and fish (Did I mention the fish?) and it's easy to see how the Kenai seduces outdoors lovers. Jenny and Kim sometimes take weekends out of the city, drive down to their home on the water (home sounds more accurate than cabin since it is a two-story house), and take in the solitude of winter when things are snowy and iced up. Their development isn't set up for winter use, which is a shame, so they have to improvise for water to get through those days in comfort, but the wilderness still beckons in the off-season when the fish are pretty much on vacation.

"It was always a dream to have a place down here," Kim said. That's a pretty common dream shared by thousands of Alaskans, but only a select group of them have the finances and opportunity to make it work out.

Putting time in on the river not only makes you smarter about fishing and sharper about driving the boat so you don't clip any rocks; the more you are out there the more likely you are to catch fish, naturally, but also to have close encounters with the wild animals. Everyone wants to see wildlife in the wild in Alaska, but it is definitely a be-careful-what-you-wish-for deal. Like Bob Sizemore who had special permission to fish in that narrow channel only to find himself face-to-face with a bear, a couple of years ago Jenny saw something that resembled an outtake from an *Animal Planet* video.

She was out fishing in the boat and as she relaxed the placid scene was interrupted by a moose tearing out of the woods and plunging into the water. It frantically began swimming across the river. Only seconds behind the moose was a grizzly bear in hot pursuit as if it was a police car chasing a suspect in a crime. The bear hit the brakes and screeched to a halt at water's edge, then stood up showing its full height. OK, time to get out of there. Jenny realized she and the moose had the same plan. The moose got away and Jenny motored away. Nobody followed up with the bear.

Dinnertime approached and our couple-of-hours fishing trip was over. I was the only one who caught silvers to keep. "Good thing we brought Lew with us," Jenny said. I laughed inwardly, thinking back to those fishless days with Harry Gaines and what he might say to me on a day when I was the only one in a boat who caught salmon.

Back at the house (where I did take note of a "Fisherman's Paradise" sign on a hallway wall) we talked about a recent huge windstorm that shook up Anchorage with winds ranging from sixty miles per hour in town, knocking out electrical power for thousands in residential neighborhoods, to a high of around one hundred miles per hour in the nearby Hillside. Still part of Anchorage, the Hillside area features houses built in the foothills of the Chugach Mountain Range. At an elevation a few thousand feet higher than the city, that section usually receives more snow in a snowstorm and stronger winds in a windstorm.

In town my daughter Alison and grandsons Malachi and Britain lived by candlelight from a Tuesday to Saturday. Interestingly, if we had brought fish back from that trip on the river with Cody it would have spoiled because Alison lost everything in her freezer and refrigerator. Kim and Jenny lost power in their south Anchorage home, too, but they have a backup generator and that rescued their freezer jam-packed with salmon and halibut. Friends called looking for help, wanting to drop off food in their protected freezer, but Kim and Jenny couldn't come to their aid because of all the fish stored on the premises. As it turned out, the timing of the request was just a little off; Kim was going to Texas shortly to see her mother and was bringing fish on the plane. A couple of weeks later and there would have been freezer space galore. Although it's not clear if Kim's older relatives saw the gesture in such a way, her bringing fish that was caught on the Kenai Peninsula wasn't much different from what Brian Walker and Don Hancock were trying to do subsistence fishing—sharing the bounty with the elders who couldn't fish for themselves.

Kim was wondering how much Delta charged for luggage checked because the fish heading south to the Lower 48 was going to be heavy.

The next morning we headed out for round two of fishing around Mile 14 and the general vicinity, though before we could unmoor from the dock we saw an eagle land on top of a nearby tree. The eagle of the day was accounted for already.

Given the carnage on highways it's kind of amazing from the perspective of adulthood that the United States let me and the millions of others take to the roadways with a driver's license at the age of sixteen. Most of us survive it, at least. Many of the principles of driving a twenty-foot boat are the same, but many are not, like parallel parking.

The first time I ever drove a boat was kind of a spontaneous occasion at an outdoor writers' conference when a manufacturer showed up with new models to test-drive. I ended up behind the wheel going pretty fast on a lake with a manufacturer's rep and some unsuspecting passenger alongside. We took a few laps around the water and I innocently asked about the brakes. There were no brakes. The boat driver was just supposed to ease up on the gas pedal and gradually slow down. Well, by the time I heard that it was too late to dock on that go-around. Everyone, from the boat passengers, to those on shore, thought I was coming in for a landing, but I knew I was going too fast, so I turned the steering wheel, shot past, and made another loop. I actually knew what I was doing, but scared the daylights out of everyone else. By the time I came around again I was going quite a bit slower and was able to ease that baby up to the dock. No one fainted or threw up and I didn't gouge any chunks out of the side of the boat, so I thought it was a pretty successful trip all around.

However, that experience did allow me to identify with Kim when she talked about a learning curve driving their boat on the Kenai.

"Learning to drive the boat was a brand-new challenge," she said. "The wind makes a difference. The current makes a difference. I've been picking it up steadily over the last three years." It was comforting to know that I wasn't acting as the adult supervisor while Kim was still on her learner's permit. One characteristic shared by all boats bought for use on the Kenai River is a flat bottom with almost no draft. Jenny said this boat could cruise along in just two-and-a-half feet of water because of that.

Jenny took to fishing a lot earlier in life than Kim took to boat driving. As a youngster she fished frequently with her father in the Fort Lauderdale area where she grew up. Fishing saltwater is different from fishing freshwater, if only because the saltwater is the vast ocean and you may be out of sight of land when fishing, and you are likely to be fishing for different species.

Most of the fishing Jenny and Kim do on the Kenai River is typical sportfishing on rod and reel, but during the openings for subsistence sockeye salmon fishing they not only dipnet for their own share of the harvest, but take out friends so they can net their limits of red salmon. Using the boat is much easier than the Brian Walker family way of gathering fish through the Kenai Walk. You still have to net them, but the physical effort of getting to the fish and transporting the net is ameliorated by the boat's aid.

One of Kim Killion's favorite things to do while out fishing on the Kenai River is driving the boat, a task that sometimes risks hypothermia in the chilly Alaskan air.

"We took twenty-one people out," Kim said. "We took three at a time, sometimes four. We netted close to 270 fish with them. We were pretty whipped. We were going through twenty gallons of gas a day." Some of those friends brought gasoline to help out, and they took out all the friends before they fished for themselves. Alaska friends from work, friends from out of town, but obviously no friends from out of state because dipnetting is a resident-only fishery and that would be illegal. "That is a lot of fish," Kim said.

When the red runs are at their peak, the fish are so thick in the river they can be found easily. Once again, as those fishing on the beach at the mouth of the river know, it is all timing. If there are fish you can catch a substantial number. If there are few fish you can fish until you drop and you are lucky if you ever get more than one fish at a time in the net.

"There were days when we were pulling them in so fast I couldn't get them in the fish hold," Kim said, "and this fish hold holds sixty fish."

As favors to everyone, Kim and Jenny did all of that first and after everyone else had come through they still had no fish to bring home. "Then we went out on our own," Kim said.

For our second try on the river together it was a fabulously blue-sky day. The temperature dropped into the thirties overnight, but it was rising past forty as we set out for another couple-hour adventure. It was Sunday and Kim and Jenny could only stay out for a limited amount of time. They had some work to do at the house before returning to Anchorage for another workweek.

That morning they told me about the only person I had ever heard of falling out of a boat on the Kenai River. No guide has ever said they had anyone go overboard by accident (we're excluding Dan Myers here, the guide who dove in to wrestle that ninety-pound king salmon). It takes a certain amount of practice and a certain touch to set the hook in a king salmon. Guides will tell you to hit it hard at the right moment to set it, but one day a guest from Texas was aboard and he hooked a king. In his effort to set the hook he yanked so hard and pulled back so far that he knocked himself into the river. Man overboard.

He was wearing hip waders, and they didn't protect him sufficiently. He got soaked. "He was so cold we could hardly get him back into the boat," Jenny said. "He didn't lose the rod, though. It was like he was trying to fillet the fish before he caught it. He was yelling, 'I still got the rod! I still got the fish!'"

Like so many other Kenai River aficionados, Kim and Jenny worked their way up to the summer home. Jenny talks of the days of looking for campground space, then leasing a place, then using an RV park. When they heard about their development going up, "We were the first two to put down earnest money. We wanted a spot. How much better can it get? There are a lot of fun people in the neighborhood."

She didn't have to sell me. I was ready to move in year-round, never mind just summers.

"This is our hobby," Jenny said. "This is our passion and our getaways. We don't mind sharing it with friends. We don't have a lot of hassle."

It being Southcentral Alaska, sunshine can often be at a premium and we were lucky it wasn't overcast and rainy, a common occurrence that fishermen must deal with on the river. When it is sunny, as it was this day, and you are moving about on the river, you sometimes are beneficiaries of stupendous scenery in the distance, in addition to the water, trees, and wildlife in close proximity. On this day we had a breathtaking view of Mount Spurr, an 11,070-foot peak in the Tordrillo Mountains on the Kenai Peninsula. I can stare at mountains like that as long as I can stare at the waters of the Kenai.

At one time or another during the summer, sometimes only in glimpses, depending on the cooperation of the sky, from afar I had seen 4,134-foot Mount Augustine, which is in Cook Inlet, and 9,150-foot Mount Redoubt, just west of Cook Inlet. Besides being snow-covered mountains, along with Spurr, the trio of peaks has another major thing in common. All of them are volcanoes and each of them erupted once during the years I lived in the state. In Anchorage at different times, years apart, we had ash rain down upon us as if it was water. Not that it looked or felt anything like water. The ash resembled sand in consistency except that it was gray. The most notable way the ash interfered with our lives was shutting down all air traffic. The gritty ash could have brought down jetliners by clogging their engines and it was too risky to take off or land based on which way the wind might be blowing.

When seen the way Jenny, Kim, and I viewed Spurr that morning, the mountain was a welcome decoration to the horizon and looked harmless. Another day, though, with ash spewing into the sky, it could appear as a deadly menace. There were no eruptions during my Kenai River summer and none were expected anytime soon. No one could blame the king problem on ash polluting the river—that seemed like one of the few things that could be ruled out. But it was inevitable that all three of them, Spurr, Augustine, and Redoubt would one day blow their tops again.

There were no quick fish bites that morning. "Fish, where are you?" Kim said aloud after a little while.

Jenny was happy about the good weather, recalling a trip with Kim and a friend named Kevin. The bite was slow, but they caught some rainbow trout. The weather that day was nasty with wind and rain. "I was ready to call it a day," Jenny said, "then we took a break and ate lunch with a shore fire. That was nice. It made the rest of the day bearable."

Being Sunday it was a non-guide day, so the others in the boats on the river were private fishermen, mostly area residents. A couple of neighbors of Jenny and Kim were out and waved to them. Kim thought it would be more advantageous to move the boat to another spot, Fallin' In Hole. Jenny was not in favor of emulating the activity that probably was at the root of the naming of that place. "No baptizing," she said.

I could understand her warning when I was told a second tale of a friend going overboard. Hard to believe that they had two. This was their friend Ron. A number of Septembers ago they were out fishing with friends from Seattle. "Ron is a type A kind of guy," Jenny said. "We were flying down the river and it's foggy. He just wanted to get to the fishing spot before anyone else claimed it." So Ron eased the boat into the preferred location and idled it as he repaired to the back of the boat to lift anchor and drop it in.

"Ron picks it up and throws it and he goes right in after it," Jenny said. "He threw it in and there it goes." The advice he received was simple: You're supposed to let go. "He was chilly."

After watching me catch the silvers the day before and not getting a bite starting out this morning, Kim was not pleased. "We can't get skunked again," she said of her and Jenny. A good hit followed and she was reeling steady when the fish spit the hook. At least the fish had the courtesy to ignore Kim's interest, rude as it was, before taking up too much of her time.

It had been only a week earlier when Jenny hooked a fish that fought like Mike Tyson and she knew it was a big one. It might as well have been a submarine, though, because after ten minutes of reeling, she still had not seen it. It was about that long before it splashed and longer before it came in. "That was a fun fight," Kim said. "I was going 'Fight, fight, fight.' It was all over the place. This side, that side." Given that it was a fourteen-pound coho, it was all worth it.

A minute later, Kim hooked a fish and worked it to the side of the boat. Jenny was ready with the net, reached over the side, and couldn't get it. The fish escaped. It looked like a big silver "Oh darn," Kim said. "I'm actually being a sport playing catch and release today. That was still fun, but that would have been a nice one to bring into the boat."

"If you caught every one you hooked, it wouldn't be fishing." Jenny added, "I just couldn't get to him." Kim laughed and said, "That was a fire drill."

The friendly seal came back to scare the fish away, and to swallow every one he could, too. There goes the neighborhood. There were a couple more hits, a humpy here and there, but no silvers this day when we quit.

Not that you would catch me complaining. Two fine trips on the river,

A good day of fishing on the Kenai River is represented by this bucket of silver, or coho, salmon.

a couple of silvers in the freezer from the day before. Since the odds were against me moving into that development anytime soon I just hoped that I would get the chance to come back there to fish again.

We were all headed back to Anchorage that afternoon, but not all in the same vehicle. Jenny and Kim needed to take care of odds and ends before going home, so I headed out before them in my rental car. The last thing Kim said to me as I started the engine was, "Drive safe."

That was fully my intention. Too bad things didn't work out that way. There is only one route from Anchorage to Soldotna to follow and I have driven on that two-lane highway many dozen times. It was sunny out. The pavement was dry. But less than an hour into the drive to Anchorage, going about fifty miles per hour, my car hit a rough spot in the road that I never saw, and it threw the vehicle into the metal guard railing on the right. As I hit the brakes I scraped the railing for several yards.

I braked and while still trying to stop and regain complete control of the car, I saw the opening to a large dirt parking lot on my right. I cut the wheel quickly to turn in, but the car didn't respond as sharply as I expected. Near the entrance to the lot I ran into a concrete abutment and that impact tossed me into the culvert right behind it. The car continued beyond the hole and as it slowed all of the way down I was able to guide it out of the way of other cars at the back of the lot, where it conked out and could not be restarted.

I was not injured, except for being perhaps slightly bruised from contact with the steering wheel as the seat belt held me more or less in place. The prognosis was a lot worse for the car. The right side had paint peeled off from the guard rail. The front end was partially caved in and the radiator was dead with steam hissing out of it. The car was in no condition to be driven and it didn't matter anyway because it wouldn't start. Due to some fluke I had totaled my rental car. I surveyed the surroundings. There were no houses or buildings or businesses of any kind anywhere nearby. There were a handful of cars parked in the lot, where a trail led away for hikers.

"I could be here a while," I thought. "Here" was about ninety miles from Anchorage. The thing to do, I knew, was to call the Alaska State Police on my cell phone. That's when I discovered how much in the middle of nowhere I was. No signal where I sat in the car. I got out and walked around the parking lot. Still no signal. I walked up to the edge of the highway and tried again. I got a ring and answer from the state troopers, but after about half a sentence the phone cut off. I tried again and got another half sentence out to the dispatcher. After a third time of being cut off after uttering a few words I think I got part of my message across and heard the man say a trooper would be coming out to me.

I thought. But I wasn't really sure that's what I heard, so when a couple came out of the woods at the end of their hike I approached then, clued them in about my mini-disaster, and asked if their phones worked. The woman tried her phone. No dice. The guy said he knew the area well and this was pretty much a cell phone blackout area. However, my good Samaritan, Kyle Jensen, a Kenai firefighter, said there was a place about a mile back where one could pull in and drive slightly up a hill and get reception there. He knew because he had stopped there before.

Kyle gave me a ride and I called the troopers back. They had received my semi-Morse code message before and someone was on the way. I called the rental car company and believe it or not they put me on hold! Knowing the trooper was on his way, I couldn't waste time like that. I called my old pal Kim and quickly filled her in on the crash and my whereabouts and asked if they could stop for me when they were on their way to Anchorage. Then Kyle deposited me back at the wrecked car and as he drove off he said, "Be safe."

Mr. State Policeman came, checked everything out, and informed me that the office had also notified the rental car company. Good deal. He said that usually when an accident like this happened the person was stuck on the premises until a tow truck arrived from Anchorage a few hours later and gave the driver a ride back to town. If I could get a ride otherwise, more power to me; I didn't have to wait with the thrashed vehicle.

Luckily for me Kim and Jenny came along within another twenty minutes or so and gave me a lift back to Anchorage. "Remember when you said, 'Drive safe?'" I said to Kim. "It didn't work."

I did make it back to Anchorage with only one black and blue mark. I never saw the car again.

THE LAST SILVER TRIP—OR NOT

The plan was to take one last silver salmon fishing trip with Reuben Hanke in the waning days of September. The regulations governing fishing for coho salmon on the Kenai River have changed several times over the years. The limit amounts have shifted, but the three-fish-per-day silver limit was in effect for September, which was pretty promising.

There were times when I lived in Anchorage that the silver season officially ended October 1, but that was no longer in effect. In some ways it was almost a defacto demarcation as the end of the season because by October in this region it is getting on to winter and it may well be below freezing early in the morning. School has started and everyone is looking ahead to skiing and not behind at fishing, except for the seriously hard-core angler. There is so little activity it doesn't matter if the occasional wacko oblivious to the weather wants to spend time on the river in October.

"I haven't had a call for October in I-don't-know-how-long," Reuben said.

My season finale silver trip was going to be on September 29, but days before that it was apparent such a journey was in jeopardy. During late September it started raining in Southcentral Alaska and day after day it poured, the inch count from rain mounting up as if it were a snow count instead. Worse, the rains were accompanied by devastating winds.

At one point the state shut down all public boat launch areas with access to the Kenai River because of flooding. The area where I first saw the cold-weather anglers in April was under water. Bings Landing, where I had set off from a couple of times over the summer, was closed. The river gushed over the banks and was running through parking lots.

The outlook was bleak. "I could launch a boat from my driveway," Reuben informed me. "OK, I'm game," I said. It was not an offer, but a lament. I would need an ark to even make it to the fish camp because the dirt access road at the end of Big Eddy Road was under water.

Reuben's tiny office on the property has a few steps leading up to it. The steps were under water and the water rose to just slightly below the door frame. The building barely escaped having water sneak into the work area. If Reuben had the door open, though, he could have fished from the office. He actually saw salmon floating past in the driveway. "You might have as good a chance of catching a fish in the pasture behind my house as on the river right now," he said. I was game for trying that too, but once again that was not an invitation, but words accompanied by a deep sigh. "There are no defined riverbanks," Reuben said. At the height of this flood, proving they were everywhere, there were humpies swimming past his office.

When you live on a river some day the river is going to flood you. It had happened before to Reuben and he knew it might happen again as long as he stayed. During a 1995 Kenai River flood, he said, his kids actually did catch silver salmon in the yard. "The 1995 flood was almost identical," he said, "and they said that was a 100-year flood. Three years ago the river was running through the yard. You see those floods with some regularity." Generally, Reuben expects a flood of some sort from the river going over the banks every five years.

"With rivers, that's the thing," Reuben said. "Everything I have came from that river, so if once in a while it takes a little bit back, that's just the way it goes."

So I was not going to take a last shot at silvers out of the Harry Gaines Kenai Fishing guide service because it would have been a bummer to end the summer by drowning. But that didn't mean I couldn't be one of the diehards willing to fish in October.

The Kenai River has many personalities. Sometimes the water is placid. Sometimes the water churns. Solo fishermen wearing waders step a couple of feet into the swiftly moving water. Other fishermen prefer being rowed by guides in areas where motorized travel is prohibited.

PACKING UP FOR WINTER

Bob Penney was shutting down his Kenai River house for the season the first week in October. He was off to warmer climes for the winter, probably splitting time between California and Mexico before returning once again to his favorite place on earth the following May.

For him it had been a discouraging summer, primarily because of the lack of king salmon in the river. The low returns were perplexing, alarming, and there was no way to know if things would improve in 2013. He did not catch a king salmon to keep and put in the freezer in 2012. He was talking to politicians and fishery experts constantly, trying to determine what was going wrong with the species, what was the source of the problem, and trying to work on solutions on how to best protect the salmon.

Fish come first was his ongoing belief and he repeated it often during the summer of 2012. It was possible that what we saw in the Kenai River with king salmon this year was the beginning of a downward cycle and that for another four or five years the king salmon runs would be abnormally low until weather patterns, ocean temperatures, or something changed. Maybe they would come back strong the next year, or maybe they would not come back strong for some years. Hopefully, they would come back strong sometime.

There was some good news out there to use as an optimistic guideline. The Pacific salmon population had crashed in Washington, Oregon, and California some years before, but their numbers were up again and fishing was improving again in those states.

In the meantime, before he departed Alaska for the season, Penney, Ricky Gease, the executive director of the Kenai River Sportfishing Association, and others involved in the organization of the annual Kenai River Classic were pretty much resolved to implement big changes as the twentieth anniversary fund-raising event loomed. As a result of the low king salmon runs and the uncertainty of what was going to happen in the near future, plans were being set in motion to shift tournament dates.

Starting in 2013, the idea was to hold the Classic in August instead of early July and focus the entrants' fishing on silvers instead of kings. If this year was any example they couldn't count on kings being available and they couldn't count on being allowed to fish anything but catch and release. So instead of being presented with such a discomfiting situation, it made sense to take kings out of the equation altogether. Even if silver runs were down, there would still be a lot more silvers available.

"We had seventy-one paid participants this year at the Classic, and some invitees, and we fished for two days," Penney said. "We caught eight kings in two days and released them all. If that isn't a warning bell, if that isn't a siren, you'd better pay attention. So it's my opinion, as far as I'm concerned, it should be set in stone that we're not going to fish for kings anymore. If it changes and the runs come back, we can change back, but I'm very strong in my feelings. I'm not going to be part of anything that targets king salmon until king salmon are back to where they should be."

Of course Penney's pet peeve is what he perceives as a past leniency giving preference to commercial set-netters to catch kings when the sports fishery has been shut down or limited. But no one can argue that the commercial fishermen did not suffer mightily in 2012 due to the absent kings along with sportfishing guides. Whether the figure was final or could be changed, it was estimated by the state Department of Commerce that the impact on commercial fishermen because of the closures during

Mike Campbell, a longtime Alaskan, always wanted to fish for rainbow trout during the second run and did so, although the waves on Skilak Lake were so strong during the return to shore he had to hold on to Kevin Thurman's cataraft so it didn't drift away before the guide could retrieve his vehicle.

the season was $16.8 million, though there were other areas that could contribute to additional losses.

The financial ripple effect from an absence of king salmon in Alaska has wide-ranging tentacles.

THE LAST DANCE

You should see them, Kevin Thurman had been telling me for months. The big rainbow trout come into the Kenai River in October. I was a believer and I was coming back. The real question, after the September flooding, was whether or not the Kenai River would have me back. Could we even put into the river?

Don't worry, Kevin kept telling me. The fishing will be good, he said. My friend Mike Campbell was initially skeptical. My partner for this fishing excursion figured there was no chance we would make it onto the river.

I kept telling him the guide assured me we would be OK. Mike had lived in the state for thirty-five years and always wanted to try fall rainbow fishing on the Kenai, but never went.

At a last consultation with Thurman the day before departure, we learned it was possible to fish, but getting onto the river remained a challenge that had to be creatively tackled. All the usual launch spots were closed, so Kevin was going to take us onto the river via Skilak Lake.

It was a sneaky approach and others obviously knew it as well. There were about a dozen trailers and trucks parked in the lot. The night before we had rain mixed with snow and the air temperature was around thirty degrees in the morning. Happily, Thurman wasn't one of those crack-of-dawn guys so we waited until daylight-plus to head onto the water.

Thurman had just pulled his truck and cataraft into the lot when he heard someone hailing him from the lake. The man, who Kevin knew, pulled as close to shore as he could, tossed Thurman a set of keys and asked him to bring his truck down to the launch ramp. It seemed the fellow had a slight problem—his boat was taking on water and he had to keep circling to keep it afloat.

Kevin drove the man's truck up to the edge of the water and he made a run for it, gunning the boat right up onto the trailer. Once safely on land, the man wandered over to talk. "I owe you, man," he said to Thurman. It turned out the man hadn't gone fishing at all, but was hunting bears. He spotted a bear the day before and this time returned with his rifle. If his boat hadn't let him down he fully expected that, "I would have been skinning a bear" at that moment.

Thurman put the cataraft into the water and tied it to a tree. Then we set off on the lake, which was minimally choppy. There were no big waves. We had to cross a few hundred yards of open water to reach the connection to the river, which happened to be right at the usual red-hot rainbow trout spot we would have approached from the other direction under normal circumstances.

In July Thurman had a fishing trip with a mother, a twelve-year-old girl, and a younger boy, somewhere between six and eight years old. There were so many sockeyes splashing around, red against the darker color of the water, that they were calling them tomatoes.

"For his years," Thurman said, "the boy was a really good fisherman. It was rainy and it was crappy, but the fishing was pretty good. All of a sudden, wham! A fish hit and it whipped that rod right out of his hands. Gone. I watched it go upriver. The boy sat there in disbelief. That was the first time that had ever happened. It went like a freight train."

Mike asked Kevin what was his favorite time to fish. "Right now," he said. "There are some big 'bows here, but it's just that there is a lot of water."

The fish were there, but it wasn't certain we would be able to get to them. The river was over its banks in many areas and ordinarily the rainbow trout would be more hemmed in on a narrower river, perhaps right up against the banks. But the banks were no longer walls. They were covered in water and the fish might have gone over too.

A rainbow hit my hook. I reeled in the first fish of the day. It wasn't a long one, but it was pudgy. Thurman called it a little football. "These are twice as fat as they were last month," he said. Yes, the rainbow trout of October are bigger than earlier in the summer. Yet it was quite clear as we moved around that the remnants of the flooding (the public launches would reopen in a couple of days because the water was receding) still affected and reconfigured the terrain. We really were lucky that we got out onto the water at all that day.

"Look!" Kevin said. There was a loon within several feet of us. The bird seemed as surprised as we were and scuttled a bit farther away immediately. Rarely do loons come within a half-dozen feet of people like that. Loons are gorgeous birds. They generally resemble ducks, but the ones we see in Alaska have single-colored heads, black in this case, with black and white checks along their backs, a white belly, and red eyes. They weigh around twelve pounds. This was probably the closest I'd ever been to a loon and it appeared bigger than I would have thought.

"I like it whenever I see a loon in the area," Thurman said. "It's not there by accident. It's there because there are fish." Loons can dive up to 200 feet (guess that's the point at which they get the bends) and can hold their breath for ninety seconds, or roughly the same as Michael Phelps (I think).

There was a dramatic change in the environment. More mountains in the distance seemed covered with snow and in many areas all of the leaves were off the trees. I was wearing a heavier coat now than I had used over the summer and I wore gloves the entire day. Thurman figured most of the fishermen who belonged to the vehicles in the parking lot were after silvers, but not us.

It seemed as if something was tickling my line, but I couldn't tell for sure if I had a bite. I watched the rod and asked Kevin, "What do you think?" No, he shook his head. Then the rod bent. "You've got a fish on." I reeled and shook my head. "Nah, there's no resistance." And then there was a fish on. I reeled and reeled and barely felt a pull. It was going along for the ride rather than fighting. Finally, near the boat there was resistance, but it was too late for the fish. Our second catch. Weird.

The next fish up from the deep was a Dolly Varden. Late-season dollies are as beautiful as rainbow trout and some of them are just as large. "Hello, Dolly," I said. This one had a colorful, speckled body and it was stunningly picturesque. We got another Dolly immediately afterward. "There are some fish to be had," Kevin said. "You have the most cooperative fish in the world," Mike said to me.

It was pretty quiet on the river. There was only one other boat in use in sight. We weren't fishing for silvers, we were fishing for rainbows, but we kept catching Dolly Varden. One hit my line harder and I definitely knew it was there and worked for it. Mike had a big hit. He could tell right away that this was a big fish. It was clearly bigger than any of the others and more attractive, too. There were orange dots mixed with the silver siding and it was probably the prettiest Dolly I had ever seen. "Nice colors," Mike said, "They look beautiful when they get colored up like that."

I had caught most of the early fish, but Mike hooked the biggest and joked, "I was just waiting." Another Dolly was hooked moments later. "If the water wasn't so high they'd be rainbows," Kevin said. "We'd be killing them."

For a change of pace I landed a humpy. Shades of yestermonths. I have often done my best fishing when I was looking at the scenery, barely paying attention. It's one of those deals where I theorize that the fish are waiting to catch me unawares, so if I really am unawares they will bite. Well, it works sometimes.

Thurman said this was his sixty-fifth trip of the season and that he would keep it up no matter how cold it got until the end of October. "October separates the men from the boys," he said. I was feeling tougher already. Actually, outside of my toes feeling a little frosty, I wasn't really cold.

There definitely was a lot of water wherever we parked the cataraft. You could tell it was higher than usual by how far back into the trees the water ran, even if it was lower than the peak flood stage. More water for rainbow trout to hide in. Mike brought in another fish and I was startled to hear Thurman say it was a whitefish. A whitefish. I didn't even know there were whitefish in the Kenai River. My next bite was a humpy, which didn't exactly trump a whitefish.

Humpies and Dollies and the occasional rainbow made their way to us. Mike's rod bowed and he said, "That was a pretty good hit." The fish spit the hook right at the boat after his reeling seemed complete.

"A lot of big boys have been lost at the boat," Thurman said. "That's the most critical time." He had a woman on board who lost a thirty-inch-plus rainbow and Thurman thought for sure the fish gave him the evil eye as he swam away.

Mike brought in a rainbow that splashed and jumped out of the water three times as he fought it, just the way those fish always do on the TV outdoors shows. And us without our video camera. It looked like a prime catch until we got it to the boat. "A jumper," he said. It turned out to be not very long at all, but quite fat and Mike marveled over the color and bright pink spots. Kevin released it. "Good-bye," he said. "Get bigger."

My next catch mirrored Mike's. It was a smaller sized rainbow, but it didn't engage in much of a battle. Mike captured a Dolly Varden, talking to it as he reeled. "How about that?" he said. "Come to me."

"Mike's got the hot stick," Thurman said. "This is probably the best fishing day for me in four years," Mike said.

The cataraft ran over a fish. It was a dead humpy and the body was decaying. It didn't look much better after the boat hit it either. "Anyone want any sushi?" Kevin said.

Whatever we were doing it was magic as far as attracting Dolly Varden. Those fish were hungry. I brought another one in and Kevin said, "We're killing the Dollies." Actually, we weren't killing anything. Every single fish of every type we caught we released. Just to support Thurman's comment in the abstract, Mike caught another Dolly.

The sun penetrated the clouds and we noticed a couple of eagles perched in a tree. I had seen more eagles than king salmon all summer and almost as many eagles as humpies. Well, maybe I was going overboard there.

We didn't have a real time limit set on how long we were going to stay out on the river, but after a few more shifts of location the fishing seemed to dry up and a foreboding wind rose. We had caught rainbow trout, humpy salmon, whitefish, and Dolly Varden. Our menu was almost as varied as Red Lobster's. But that wind was sending us a warning. From a mild breeze it grew in intensity and although that would not ordinarily be a major problem on the river, the problem was that we had to recross wide-open Skilak Lake to return to the parking lot.

Thurman had consulted a weather report and expected some wind. The forecast was for five-to-ten miles per hour. We could handle that with ease. There was only one problem. Those numbers seemed to be an underestimate of reality. It was 2 P.M., the fish had seemingly stopped biting, and those wind gusts were increasing. "This ain't five-to-ten," Thurman said.

We talked it over briefly. If we were smart we would probably put up the rods and start heading back in. "You've got to know when to call it off," Thurman said. He wasn't asking us so much as telling us that it was time to go before the wind truly began howling and made the several-hundred-yard journey across the open water a dangerous ride.

We battened down the hatches, almost literally. Rods were stored beside our seats. Backpacks and the like were stored in a closed box. Kevin's enormous tackle box was placed on a seat in the middle of the cataraft. Mike and I put up our hoods, spinning our backs to the forward end of the boat and the wind.

It only took seconds before it was apparent that the five-to-ten-miles-per-hour wind talk was a complete myth. The wind was howling, and we were chugging across three-foot waves that tossed us about a little. Skilak Lake's surface was pretty much rolling hills of whitecaps. "This is a hurricane," Thurman said. Not literally, but we were definitely going into thirty-plus-miles per hour winds. He took it slow and we rode up and down on the waves.

He asked if I was OK and I said, "Given that I once was on a much bigger lake with much bigger waves on a foggy afternoon where the guide couldn't figure out the way home . . . until you top that I'm OK."

Mike and I could feel the spray hitting our heads and backs, but looking at Kevin, stone-faced while he was lashed in the face by wind and water I asked if *he* was OK. "I'm just in captain mode," he said.

"I feel like I'm on *The Deadliest Catch*," Mike said.

Since we were on a raft I thought maybe it was like being on Kon-Tiki.

It was a fifty-five-minute roller-coaster ride that on another day might have taken twenty minutes. The cataraft was very stable and didn't at any time seem at risk from the wave action. The approach to the launch, however, took delicate action. The water was rough and Kevin had to figure out how to place the boat just so in order for us to jump out and hold it in a place where it would be easy to slide onto to his trailer when he brought it over. He dumped us out in foot-deep water and handed over a rope to hold the cataraft steady.

Mike and I were right in front of a boater's warning sigh, making sure the craft didn't escape into the whitecapped water. It was a sign erected for a day just like this, purposely designed to scare people into prudence. It read: "Lake water originates from glacial melt and is 10 degrees centigrade. If you capsize your chances of survival are poor. Be prepared to spend the night. It is better to come home late than not at all."

When I finished reading the alert sign, I gazed out at Skilak Lake with its roiling waters and roaring wind. The gateway to the Kenai River seemed far away. It was October in Alaska and the river was telling us it was time to go home for the season.

About the Author

Lew Freedman has fished for salmon and rainbow trout on the Kenai River for about a quarter of a century. He lived in Alaska for seventeen years, and was sports editor of the *Anchorage Daily News*. The winner of more than 250 journalism awards, Freedman is the author of more than sixty books, many of them on Alaska subjects.

Among Freedman's Alaska titles are *Thunder on the Tundra: Football Above the Arctic Circle*, and as coauthor, *Bradford Washburn, An Extraordinary Life: The Autobiography of a Mountaineering Icon*.

Freedman lives in Indiana with his wife, Debra.